AF594711

Praise for *Journey into His Heart*

"Barbara Heil's beautiful spiritual memoir, *Journey into His Heart*, is an inspiring witness to the fullness of life that comes from a radical obedience to Christ and His Holy Spirit. I count myself among the many whose lives have been touched by her choice to follow the Spirit's promptings into the Catholic Church. May Barbara's witness to the Lord's calling to her heart touch your heart and encourage you!"

—Bishop Scott Bullock, Diocese of Rapid City

"Barbara's story demonstrates the amazing fruitfulness of a life laid down in radical obedience to the Lord. This book is an invitation for Catholics to discover the simplicity of the gospel and the fire of the Holy Spirit and for all Christians to discover the riches of the fullness of truth in the Catholic Church."

—Dr. Mary Healy, Professor of Sacred Scripture, Sacred Heart Major Seminary, Detroit; Member, Pontifical Biblical Commission

"As personal as it is engaging, *Journey into His Heart* is the moving story of how a Pentecostal missionary became Catholic. May all readers be inspired by Barbara's radical obedience to Jesus and the kinds of blessings He grants in response to such obedience."

—Fr. Mathias Thelen, Cofounder and President, Encounter Ministries

"This is the amazing—and enjoyable—story of one woman's journey from a difficult childhood, through conversion to Christ and major involvement in Pentecostal mission work, into the Catholic Church. I know Barbara and have heard her teach and preach many times, and I'm grateful that she is now sharing her story with all of us."

—Dr. Ralph Martin, S.T.D., Director of Graduate Programs in the New Evangelization, Sacred Heart Major Seminary, Detroit

"Barbara Heil has written a powerful book on how Christ led her into the Catholic Church. Her journey, led by the Holy Spirit, is an inspiration to all of us! This book is a must-read for anyone who desires to be an evangelist!"

—Deacon Steve Greco, President, Spirit Filled Hearts Ministry

Journey into His Heart

Barbara Heil

Journey into His Heart

How the HOLY SPIRIT *Led Me into the* CATHOLIC CHURCH

Foreword by JEFF CAVINS

SOPHIA INSTITUTE PRESS
Manchester, New Hampshire

Copyright © 2025 by Barbara Heil

Printed in the United States of America. All rights reserved.

Cover design by LUCAS Art & Design, Jenison, MI.

On the cover: Woods in Uetliberg, Zürich, Switzerland; photo by Marco Meyer / Unsplash (marco-meyer-8Fn_Fh0X5AY-unsplash.jpg).

Unless otherwise noted, Scripture references are taken from the Catholic Edition of the Revised Standard Version of the Bible, copyright 1965, 1966 by the Division of Christian Education of the National Council of the Churches of Christ in the United States of America. Used by permission. All rights reserved.

Excerpts from the English translation of the *Catechism of the Catholic Church* for use in the United States of America copyright © 1994, United States Catholic Conference, Inc.—Libreria Editrice Vaticana. English translation of the *Catechism of the Catholic Church: Modifications from the Editio Typica* copyright © 1997, United States Conference of Catholic Bishops—Libreria Editrice Vaticana.

No part of this book may be reproduced, stored in a retrieval system, or transmitted in any form, or by any means, electronic, mechanical, photocopying, or otherwise, without the prior written permission of the publisher, except by a reviewer, who may quote brief passages in a review.

Sophia Institute Press
Box 5284, Manchester, NH 03108
1-800-888-9344
www.SophiaInstitute.com

Sophia Institute Press® is a registered trademark of Sophia Institute.

paperback ISBN 979-8-88911-580-9
ebook ISBN 979-8-88911-581-6

Library of Congress Control Number: 2025936698

First printing

To my husband, Jeff,
who kept encouraging me to write it all down

Contents

Foreword

You most likely picked up this book because you are searching for something deeper, something more substantial in your relationship with God. You are not that unusual; many people seek God: some seek Him in the Bible, some look for Him in philosophy or in New Age teachings, and still others look for Him in the experiences of this world.

All the people you pass on the street and see at the store are on some journey toward what they hope will make them happier. Indeed, all of life is a pilgrimage; none of the people you encounter are mere mortals; they are infinitely valuable and eternal beings.

I have found that many on this journey settle into a place of comfort, a place that becomes familiar, somewhere between boredom and burnout. The human spirit was not created to be bored, nor was it created for burnout. Somewhere in between the two is a place where life can be lived with an ever-increasing sense of spiritual growth and a corresponding confidence in God!

It was Barbara Heil's hunger for God and refusal to stay at the same level of growth that propelled her to that next level of intimacy with God. As you read her story, you may see some common denominators in your life that hopefully will bring you to a place of decision as well. It takes faith to guide us to the next level; it takes hope to draw us ever closer to God, and it takes charity to execute God's will.

Barbara and I have something in common: we pursued a deeper relationship with the Lord while being strapped with responsibilities in a community of faith that may not have understood the movement of our hearts. You may find yourself in the same situation as Barbara, so read carefully her insight into her adventure in spiritual growth.

Pope St. John Paul II understood the progression of pilgrimage and made these remarks on his General Audience of August 11, 1999:

> After meditating on the eschatological goal of our existence, that is, eternal life, we now reflect on the journey that leads to it. To do this, we develop the perspective presented in the Apostolic Letter *Tertio Millennio Adveniente*: "The whole of the Christian life is like a great *pilgrimage to the house of the Father*, whose unconditional love for every human creature, and in particular for the 'prodigal son' (cf. Lk 15:11-32), we discover anew each day. This pilgrimage takes place in the heart of each person, extends to the believing community, and then reaches to the whole of humanity." (no. 1)

This unique kind of pilgrimage is also known as "conversion," and this book speaks in a special way to this kind of journey. It is a journey that—for many of us—begins at the moment of Baptism.

I want to say something about the importance of the Sacrament of Baptism and its significance in your life. Perhaps you have been baptized and have been enjoying some of the fruits of Baptism. While Baptism is an initiation into the life of the Trinity, it points to even more intimacy with Jesus—namely, the

Sacrament of Confirmation and the reception of the Eucharist, the Body and Blood, Soul and Divinity of Jesus.

Moving forward in your walk with the Lord does not negate the good and fruitful things you have experienced. Those milestones and insights may be critical for your next steps, and they should be cherished. I experienced many wonderful things in my years as a Protestant pastor. I remain grateful for all I gained before coming back to the Catholic Church, and I don't believe for a moment that I would be who I am today without having gone down some of those theological and familial roads.

Saying yes to more revelation and yes to the teachings of the early Church is not a rejection of your past, nor is it a rejection of all the wonderful people in your life who have contributed to your spiritual growth. Saying yes to more revelation opens your heart to the experiences and insights of the giants of the Faith who have traveled before you. Saying yes to more of God is expanding your spiritual family and embracing the graces of God in a way that you desire but perhaps didn't know about! It's all good; Jesus is the Master Builder, and your heart is His sensitive project!

The change that God desires to make in your life starts first in your heart. At this point in your journey, it may be quiet; others might not even know what is stirring in your spirit. God may have grabbed your attention with a book, a YouTube video, the witness of a friend, or the transformation of a family member.

What begins in your heart will then be nourished by the family of God, the Church. In fact, the Church will be instrumental in every step of your growth. But it doesn't stop there. What began in your heart and is nurtured by the Church finds a mission field in the world, a place where you can join with Jesus in changing the world.

I still remember the look on Barbara's face when she asked to join the Catechetical Institute at the Seminary of St. Paul. I know tenacity when I see it. I know the hunger of the heart when I encounter it. Through her tenacity and deep hunger, joined with wisdom, Barbara has reached a place of satisfying understanding. You can too!

Ask God to open your heart to receive more of Him. As you read, listen to Barbara, a sister in the Lord who heard God's voice and dared to venture out into the deep, only to find an even more challenging and satisfying walk with God!

Shalom!

Jeff Cavins
Founder of The Great Adventure
Catholic Bible Study Program

Journey into His Heart

Introduction

On a beautiful early spring day, in St. Paul, Minnesota, I found myself driving to Nativity of Our Lord Catholic Church with my oldest daughter, Sarah. It was Saturday, April 27, 2013, and I was about to receive the Rite of Confirmation in the Roman Catholic Church. I was not being confirmed in the usual way at the Easter Vigil; I had already received my First Holy Communion in Rome—with the permission of my archbishop. And now that I was back home, I was on the way to my Confirmation, all dressed up and feeling excitement and anticipation. Later, I remember telling my daughter that it was like I was driving to a wedding.

Arriving at the decision to embrace Catholicism had been difficult, even tortuous at times. I didn't know anyone who had become a Catholic after living a vibrant faith in the Pentecostal/Charismatic Evangelical world, and certainly not any missionaries or pastors or preachers who had become Catholic. I had never even heard of such a thing. At first it had even seemed wrong! I had met lots of former Catholics who came into *our* churches, but never the other way around. I examined my heart and turned it over and over again in my mind. It just didn't seem reasonable, let alone possible. But the Holy Spirit was tugging on my heart, and I kept coming back to the same prayerful decision. And it seemed so hard.

When I entered into the Catholic Church, I had no idea that anyone would care about how I had decided to become Catholic, much less want to hear about the process that led me from my charismatic Protestant church into the Roman Catholic Church. I myself was completely surprised that I was doing it!

The first time I received an invitation to give my testimony was right after I graduated from the Harry J. Flynn Catechetical Institute in St. Paul, Minnesota. After driving to a suburb outside the city, I found myself in the living room of a large house, with the room completely filled with all kinds of people. I had been thinking all day about what led me there, not just to the Church, but to that room, to those people. I spent time in prayer and then focused on remembering what had happened. Finally, the time came, and I stood to tell my story for the first time. It would not be the last.

Since then, I have told the story of my journey into the Church all across America and around the world. In most places I was given an average of forty-five minutes. How do you tell the story of your life's journey in forty-five minutes? Occasionally I would have a whole hour, but that was the exception. I had to learn to focus on the highlights, sharing not just how I came to the Church, but how I came to Christ, and when sharing my story, I chose not to focus on thorny theological issues but on the journey itself. My entering the Catholic Church was not about simply switching addresses of churches or denominations, but it was the continuation of the process of conversion, of finding Jesus and following Him.

The more I shared this remarkable story, the more I came to see the Spirit of God at work in my life. This was never about merely making a decision or choice. This had been chosen for me, from the earliest moments of my life, and before. He took my thirst for Him and led me. And He brought me to a home I never knew I had.

Barbara Heil
Iowa, 2025

1

Holy Thursday

The beauty of surprise is its ability to change everything.

— Author unknown

†

I had been living in a little missionary community of about a hundred people in rural Virginia for many years. We were busy serving God with a wide range of Christian endeavors, sharing the gospel of Jesus not only in America but all over the world. Thousands would attend our camp meetings, and well-known speakers would come and share the Word of God.

But most of all, we were in pursuit of His presence. We had seen that the Lord was good, and we longed for more. We lived lives of prayer and fasting, and would sing to the Lord until the Holy Spirit overflowed, transforming lives, healing hearts, and giving us a glimpse of Jesus.

One day, Catholic friends of mine, Bill and Cheryl Wolner, who were volunteers at the ministry, invited me to go to their church, St. Ann, with them. It was Holy Week, and I was happy to accept, but the only evening I had free was Thursday night. Cheryl cheerfully said, "That's great, you can come for Holy Thursday." I had never been to a Holy Thursday service in my life! We usually just focused on Good Friday and Easter Sunday, with a big old-fashioned picnic and Easter egg hunt on Easter Monday.

Quiet anticipation built up in me as the evening approached. St. Ann's was new and modern, built about a mile away from the old, historic church that was a town landmark, to meet the needs of the growing congregation. Without the lovely historic architecture, from the outside the new building looked like all the Baptist churches in the area.

Following Bill and Cheryl's lead, I went inside to participate in my first Holy Thursday Mass. I followed along with the readings and watched closely as they received the Eucharist. The whole time I wondered (and still do!) how the people around me could remain so stoic and seemingly unaffected.

Afterward, we went to a little chapel at the back of the church, just outside of the main sanctuary, where people were praying in silence before a rather large and beautiful monstrance on a little side altar. Suddenly I was overwhelmed with a sense of being in the very presence of the Lord. It was the last thing I expected—at that time in my life, I was not completely sure that Catholics were true brothers and sisters in Christ. And yet, I could not deny that the Lord was in this place. And in that moment, I never wanted to leave.

Soon, it was just me and one other older couple. As I continued praying, I began to see Jesus in the olive grove known as the Garden of Gethsemane. I could see the religious guards, angry and insulting, coming to arrest Him. I followed along as He was shoved down the hill of the Mount of Olives and around the Temple Mount, to ascend to the High Priest's court on Mt. Zion, where He was tried before Caiaphas.

I saw His face when His friends betrayed Him, and how roughly, almost savagely, He was handled and treated. I loved Him all the more for it. I kept leaning in, following what I was seeing, no longer watching, but *with* Him. Finally, I saw Him dropped into a filthy pit for the night, left in utter darkness, after being arrested, abandoned, mistreated, slapped, bullied, mocked, and beaten.

I was weeping. I wanted to be near Him. I stayed with Him and could "feel" Him as I sat across from the pit, where He was resting from His ordeal. His breathing was rough and jagged. There were wet gashes oozing water and blood all over His back and face, even His limbs. I could feel and smell the steam rise from His body in that cool, dark place. I could hear Him praying.

There was nothing I could do for Him but to just be near Him. Then He groaned and moved, and a droplet of sweat and blood mingled with the fluid of cut flesh struck my toe. I could feel it burning, but not in a painful way. I stayed, I didn't want to leave Him!

I don't know how long I stayed there with Him. Then, suddenly, someone tapped me on the shoulder.... It was like waking up. It was time to close the church and go home.

That was what I experienced on my first Holy Thursday, in the chapel at St. Ann's.

All through Good Friday and even into Easter, I still felt like I was with Him in the pit at Caiaphas's house. The place on my toe where His Blood landed on me would softly burn. For weeks, and even months, I would suddenly feel that burning sensation, and it was like I was with Jesus all over again on that Holy Thursday. I wondered why I was physically, really feeling His Blood on me.

I was, as we liked to say, "wrecked." My heart had been so moved, and I was yearning for more of God. I didn't feel like I could tell many people. How could they understand? Something had changed within me in that encounter, and I could not go back.

You might think that it was at this point that I decided to become Catholic, right there and then. But I could not! While I knew I had a deep experience of being with my Lord in His agony, I still had a long journey ahead of me before I could enter the Catholic Church. For years I had been fed so much misinformation about what Catholics believe that I had a hard time seeing them as brothers and sisters in Christ. Slowly, patiently the Holy Spirit had to work in my heart to remove the blinders and open my eyes so I could embrace and understand the traditions and teachings of the Roman Catholic Church.

Besides, I was perfectly content in my church. I was an ordained minister, with a full life, desiring only to please the Lord. He had done so much in my life. But, I was on a journey that I couldn't yet understand.

2

Jesus Saves

God's plan for your life is bigger than the circumstances.

— Louis Giglio

†

Sometimes when I meet people, they have assumptions about me. "She must have had a great life," or "Things come so easy for her," or maybe, "Wow, her family must be amazing."

The reality is that I grew up at a time when it was not uncommon for parents to use a belt or strap on their children. My father's "whippings" always ended up with me on the floor, cowering from the blows of his belt, with my mother retreating to the next room. He would get worked up to a rage, and it seemed the whipping would never end. Afterward he would yell at me to "stop crying like a baby." I would be sent to my room, unable to come back out until I was not crying. Many long nights stretched till morning before I could finally come out and get something to eat.

Sometimes, in the middle of the night, I would wake up shivering and shaking, afraid that my dad was coming into my room with his belt. For hours I would sit there, all alone in my room, wondering why my father was so unhappy with me. Was there something wrong with me? Then I would look out my window, and see a kind of vision. I called him, "The Man in the Sky." He was always there when I was sad or lonely, and sometimes even when I wasn't. He would smile at me and make me feel safe. I recall seeing him for years—he was always there, even when we moved, as we so often did.

My dad was in the U.S. Navy, and our family—my parents, my two younger brothers, and I—moved regularly, from base to base all through my childhood. We did not live near relatives or my parents' old friends. The only real community we had was "the Base," the military, and the families in my dad's squadron.

In the '60s we moved to the San Francisco Bay Area in California. My mom worked, and my brothers and I were "latchkey kids," as we each had a copy of our housekey hanging around our necks, walking to school well after our parents left for work and returning home well before they returned.

Looking back, I see now that our parents loved us as much as they could. The rages, unexpected "whacks," yelling, and regular whippings that would never be condoned today were at that time just part of life as we knew it. But there were also plenty of happy times too, with camping trips, bowling leagues, fishing expeditions, along with Girl Scouts for me and Boy Scouts for my brothers. These were the happy memories that filled our lives. I'll never forget my dad teaching me to shoot trap and skeet, and giving me my own .22 rifle on my twelfth birthday, which I proudly hung over my bed, along with my target bow and arrows.

We did not go to church. When I asked why we didn't go to church as so many of my classmates did, my dad would loudly proclaim that he was an atheist and against "organized religion," while my mom remained quiet. And that would be the end of it.

When I was twelve years old and getting ready for middle school, or junior high school as we called it back then, my dad got orders to move again, this time from Alameda, California, to Whidbey Island, Washington. My brothers and I were excited to go up north and live on a real island! On the appointed day, the movers came and everything was packed up. My dad and my two brothers drove on ahead, following the movers with all our belongings, while I spent time in Fallon, Nevada, with family friends whose kids helped me get into a lot of trouble. At the end of the summer, my parents' friends drove me to the San Francisco airport where I met up with my mom, and we flew up to Seattle together before we boarded a tiny twin propeller plane with two brand-new sailors fresh out of bootcamp who would take us on to Oak Harbor on Whidbey Island, in the Puget Sound.

It was on that plane ride that my childhood came to an abrupt end. As we flew over the most beautiful scenery imaginable, my mother told me that she and my dad were getting a divorce. She was moving to San Diego.

I asked if I could go with her, but she said a firm "No." I was stunned and sat silently as tears streamed down my face. Not another word was spoken about it, because the biggest lesson I had learned up till then was how to be quiet. I didn't even know for sure if my brothers knew about it when I got to the new house.

I wanted it not to be true. Maybe I had misheard! Everyone was just acting the same as always, just like nothing was happening. I didn't want to risk my father's anger, so I just said nothing. But then, a couple of days later I woke up, and she was gone, already heading to the airport. Now my brothers and I were in a brand-new place without a mom.

I was only twelve and in middle school. This began a particularly difficult time in life for me, and for my two younger brothers too. And so I grew up, but now I began getting into all kinds of trouble at school, acting out, ditching classes, and engaging in a whole lot of things that I'm sure would have scandalized even my parents!

My brothers and I were tasked with cleaning the house, cleaning up after two cats and a guinea pig, and cooking. My brothers fondly remember me as a tyrant, not allowing them to play with friends on Saturday until everything was done. Somehow, being the oldest, I was in charge. We did our best. Our dad was gone at "the Base" most of the time; when he was at home, he began drinking more and going out in the evenings, all the time. So, we were alone a lot. I know now that, with his wife leaving him and trying to raise three kids while working for the military, my dad did his best. Looking back, I recognize that my heartbroken and young dad, too, was acting out.

He had a lot of anger, and I hated it. He also started bringing girlfriends home. If my dad was going to be home, I tried to make sure I wasn't. I ended up spending lots of time with friends who were just as lost and wrestling with their own brokenness, and I slept at my friends' homes as often as I could, while feeling responsible for my brothers all at the same time.

My mom would call from San Diego, a place my brothers and I had never been and could not imagine. Her calls were infrequent and awkward. She did visit at Christmas. The next thing we knew, she was getting remarried.

I stayed in school and ended up living in a house near the University of Washington. It was not a good place for me to be. Everyone in the house was partying all the time. Lost, and broken, we all seemed to have banded together, trying to find our way.

And then, one day, it happened: God began to break into my life. There were these older women who kept approaching me and my friends when we were hanging around outside of the house. They would run up to us and tell us they were praying for us and hand us little slips of paper with words on them before we walked away. I was so ignorant of any religion, I didn't know they were handing out passages from the Bible until later. They would invite us to church or to church events and would even offer to drive us to these events and to pray for us. My friends and I just thought they were strange and would make loud, obnoxious jokes about them behind their backs.

One day, when I was walking alone, one of those smiling women ran up to me and handed me a tiny "wordless book." Less than two inches high and wide, the little pages were all different colors: black, red, white, and gold. It was basically construction paper except for the shiny gold page, with all the pages neatly cut and stapled together. The lady quickly explained the story that corresponded with each colored page: the black page represented the weight of carrying sin and what it does to our hearts; the red page was the Blood that Jesus shed when He died on the Cross for our sins. The white page was what happens to our heart when we surrender our lives to Christ and receive His forgiveness. Our hearts become new and we are white as snow! And the gold was the glory and goodness of God that would heal our lives and the treasures that awaited us in Heaven where we would be with God forever.

Of course, I thought she was crazy. But I kept that little book. And later, when these persistent ladies took my friends to a big youth event in a nearby town, these party friends of mine came home talking about Jesus and acting so differently—their lives were completely transformed. Something *had* happened to them; they changed and were not the same! And it scared me! *They* scared me!

Soon they were going off to meetings with those ladies all the time! But I wanted no part of it, even though what was happening in their lives was evident to all of us who knew them. My friends literally became new people! They stopped drinking, smoking, doping, cussing! They stopped sleeping around! They were smiling and happy and even singing. Singing! Soon *they* were inviting me to church!

I knew these people. The change that happened in their lives—which they claimed was because of Jesus—was real. I was actually very happy for them. But I was still uncomfortable.

"Jesus" for me had been a swear word. I'd only heard it spoken in anger, when someone was hurting me, or using me, or being abusive. I had really never heard it spoken in love before. So, when they spoke of "Jesus," it was a little bit of a trigger for me. And at first I wanted no part of it.

They invited me and invited me and invited me. I said no every time and always had an excuse. Pretty soon there were Bible studies going on in the house where I was, and other people were in the house praying. I would even hear them pray for me.

I decided it was time for me to leave. I found another place to stay, put all my belongings in two cardboard boxes, and loaded up the old station wagon with the fake wood siding. On the way across town, I decided that I at least needed to tell my best friend where I was going and that I was safe. And I knew I would find her at the one place I said I would never go.

As I pulled into the parking lot of the United Methodist Church in Woodinville, Washington, it began to rain. I was trembling and nervous when I walked through the large wooden doors that opened into a foyer that led to another set of doors. I peered through the door window trying to see where my friends were, but everyone was standing and singing, and I could not see them. So, I opened the door as quietly as possible and paced along the back of the pews before I saw them on the second row on the left-hand side. I started down the side aisle between the pews and the wall and got about halfway down when the music stopped and everyone sat down. I froze. My heart was pounding and I felt out of place. It was the 1970s and I was wearing clogs. The thin pieces of rubber on the soles of my shoes were long gone, so that each step I took in those wooden shoes on that wooden floor echoed throughout the church. Now I was embarrassed and felt my face burn. When I reached my friends, they made room for me next to Donna, my best friend, and I whispered and told her I was moving out but wanted to say goodbye.

There was a young Latino man with a microphone speaking loudly and marching back and forth on the platform, so no one noticed we were whispering. And then I got up to leave. I had to get out of there. But when I got back to the side aisle, instead of running out the back like I wanted to, I went straight to the front, in the corner where the high platform and altar met the wall. And I just stood there.

Finally, the man with the microphone stopped and asked me, "Young lady, can I help you?" and with tears streaming down my face I said, "Just get it over with. Whatever you did to them, do to me!"

And then he just left me there and continued to shout into the microphone. I don't remember anything he said. But a few moments later, several hundred other young people made their way to the front, as older men and women formed prayer teams and began to pray for us. That night I prayed "The Sinner's Prayer" and met Jesus as my Lord and Savior.

I'd been born again. I had never read a Bible. I didn't know the four spiritual laws, the Ten Commandments, or what Evangelicals call "the Roman road to salvation." All I knew was what I had been told: that God loved me, that I was born on purpose, that Jesus came to earth to die for me, and that if I would repent of my own sins, I would have this amazing new life in Christ! And I did have an amazing new life! My life truly would never be the same again!

I woke up the next day, and everything was new! Now I was the one in church all the time, at Bible studies, prayer meetings, discipleship classes, special weekend revivals. I experienced real joy! I was so thirsty for God and so grateful for His wonderful love.

I would weep whenever I heard people's testimony of how they had been lost in their sins before meeting Jesus and how their whole life had been changed forever. I marveled at His amazing, freeing love, and wept at what He had done in my life too.

Immediately, I started telling everyone, and I mean everyone, about Jesus. Imagine my surprise when I found out other people had heard of this, or even went to church, but weren't living for Him, and hadn't mentioned this great, good news to me! I would wake up singing a little song I'd heard at one of the meetings:

Everybody ought to know
Everybody ought to know,
Everybody ought to know,
Who Jesus is.

He's the Lily of the Valley,
He's the Bright and Morning Star;
He's the Fairest of ten thousand.
Everybody ought to know.[1]

I flew to California and moved in with my mother and became part of a little church in South San Diego, where I met people who would become my dear friends, Assembly of God Pastor Rev. Ken Irwin and his wife Lois, and their daughter Melody, who became my best friend and mentor in a way. They have all

1 "Everybody Ought to Know" by Harry Dixon Loes, © Copyright 1940 by Singspiration, Inc. All rights reserved. https://hymnary.org/tune/everybody_ought_to_know_loes.

passed away now, but they will always be remembered. They had a huge impact on my life! Just a short time later, and with great anticipation and excitement, I was baptized in water.

We took seriously the Great Commission to "go and tell" and to testify of what God had done in our lives! I was so hungry for God! I knew that if He could change my life, He could change anyone's life! This was the Good News!

My faith began to grow as I attended church and youth group, going to conferences and camp meetings and receiving instruction in the faith. I soon experienced the baptism in the Holy Spirit, which brought such healing and joy into my life as I encountered the Lord, surrendering to His love, in an ever-deepening way.

Also, I found a real community. I have often said that I don't know if I would have been able to remain a Christian in those early days if it had not been for the love and hospitality shown to me, and to all new believers, by people in our church.

Even though I had found joy, my new life as a new believer was not without a few bumps in the road! I didn't always feel like I could be like those "good" church people! But that began to be healed and melt away once I was at someone's house every Sunday after church, eating a homemade meal, and discussing the pastor's sermon. And I wasn't the only one! Anyone who was new, or alone, would find there was a place for them. I have many wonderful memories of one of the ladies of the church in particular who opened her home often, "Mama Slocum," reading to us about the love of God and praying with us after dinner.

I also realized The Man who had been with me when I was a little girl—it had to be Jesus! When I was a teenager, I kept thinking I must have had an imaginary friend when I was little, so I totally dismissed the experiences I'd had. But, now that I was a believer, I believed it had to be Jesus! But, why was He there?

Why was He with me, waiting for me, comforting me? As far as I knew, no one had been praying for me or interceding for me, or even worried about me! I would smile when I thought of my "Friend." And I was grateful that now I knew, Jesus Saves!

3

Go into All the World

You are a billboard for Christ.

— Fr. Mike Schmitz

†

Jesus had become the cornerstone of my entire life. How could I not love the One who loved me beyond measure? How could I not give myself, my whole life, completely to the One who had completely given Himself to me?

I would spend hours in prayer, praising God for what He was doing not just in my life but in the lives of my friends. Soon, I felt the call in my heart to serve Him with my life, and I enrolled in a Bible school in Kirkland, Washington, and began dreaming of going "on the mission field" to share Jesus. During this time, I was grounded in foundations of the Christian faith, learning many truths from Scripture, and receiving a lot of healing in my heart through the prayers of others and God's Word.

There were two things that both my church and Bible college seemed very concerned about. One was that we read the *correct* version of the Bible—which was, for them, the King James Bible. Up to that point I was so hungry for God that I would read anything I could get my hands on! But when I was in school, some very loving and well-intentioned people gave me material that taught me how wrong and sinister any version other than the King James Version of the Bible was. Now, of course "the King James" is a marvelous, poetic version of Scripture, but I would later have to "un-learn" my prejudice against any other version.

The other thing I learned was the importance of focusing our evangelistic efforts on Catholics. My church was filled with fabulous, faith-filled people who were sure that Catholics were not Christians. In those days, a great deal of anti-Catholic literature, tracts, and pamphlets were lavished on us young Christians, full of half-truths, misinformation, and outright falsehoods—many of them written by former Catholics who had not been well-formed in the faith!

At that time, it never occurred to me to question any of this. I didn't know! I just drank it all in. I wanted to be a missionary in Third World countries and reach the millions of Catholics who had never heard the gospel and were worshipping idols. Before school even officially began, I attended special seminars and received certification on Comparative Religion and how to minister effectively to Catholics and bring them out of idolatry into the *right* kind of church.

One weekend in San Diego, I had met some Pentecostal missionary evangelists who had just arrived from a mission to the Philippines; they were very faith-filled and were having great results, revival, in their meetings. They were all in! During the school break I visited their humble headquarters in Virginia, and after time spent in prayer, I began to feel called to join their community. I went back out to visit and see how it fit, and I ended up not leaving! I moved across the country to be part of their Bible school, ministry, and community. A new era had begun.

This little community in Virginia was based on what began as a summer camp for an old-fashioned Pentecostal church in Richmond. The founders, church "planters" from the Assemblies of God denomination, were originally trained as missionaries to start Spirit-filled churches all through the Mid-Atlantic states. They embraced the Spirit of Pentecost, training thousands of people who made their way to "the Campground" to press into the heart of Jesus and share the gospel with others in "word and deed." They prayed for the sick and saw many come to Christ, along with many healings, and yes, extraordinary miracles.

I was mentored by Rev. Wallace Heflin, the son of the founders, a southern Pentecostal with deep gifts of faith and healing. I owe so much to Brother Heflin, as we called him, and to his sister, Ruth, who founded the ministry house in Jerusalem. Their faith was simple but deep, and they both, with their different gifts, impacted so many lives.

It was there that I met and married my late husband Kerry, and we became part of the camp staff, living in a missionary cottage on the grounds. We lived simply, relying on monthly donors or sponsors who would give offerings—"investing" in our ministry—because they wanted to see Jesus lifted up and wanted to participate in our mission, even if they could not go themselves.

Within a few years of moving to the community in Virginia, finishing the Bible school and entering a life of devotion, learning to hear the Heart of Jesus through prayer, Scripture, fasting, and praise, I found myself on my first mission trips, participating in ministry all over the world. We traveled with our Bibles, backpacks, and a bedroll, so that we could easily go from a stadium meeting to a tiny village in the middle of Africa, loving the people, and sharing the gospel of Jesus all along the way. The Lord is faithful, and He blessed so many people with His Love, healing many as we shared the gospel.

Kerry and I were also sent to help and minister at a street mission in downtown San Diego during the AIDS epidemic. I will never forget the people I met there and the way I witnessed God working in the hearts of broken people. Many of our clientele were transvestite prostitutes, either in active drug addiction or getting too old to "work." We encountered wandering homeless persons, prostitutes young and old, and even a few times, immigrants with nowhere to go. We met entire families that were homeless but on the move. A social services team was down the street with another ministry we partnered with. We provided a free shower service, complete with toiletries; a free clothes closet where they could go in and pick out clean, donated clothes to put on after their showers; and two meals each day.

For those who were choosing to follow Jesus, we had "street" Bible studies, as well as mentoring for anyone who wanted to attend. Many times those of us on staff would be praying together in the afternoon in the main hall and dining room, and we would begin to spontaneously sing and worship King Jesus. We were "closed" until supper, and people of the streets (many who would later find out they were infected with the AIDS virus) would come and lean on the outside gates, weeping as God would touch their hearts. So many lives were touched by the love of Jesus, many transformed forever. I will never forget those days!

Back at the ministry headquarters, besides recording cable TV programming (it was the '80s!) and radio programs, we held meetings all along the East Coast and missions around the world. The ministry hosted a summer-long program of daily meetings in an old-fashioned open-air tabernacle on the campground. Thousands would travel from many nations and from all over the country to soak up the gospel preaching and teaching from notable and gifted speakers and to experience a fresh outpouring of the Spirit. I have so many wonderful memories of that old tabernacle.

God gifted me with so much during those early years. At the campground we spent hours singing and worshipping, getting "caught up" with God, learning to follow His leading and to entrust ourselves to Him. One summer in the late '80s, Ruth came from Jerusalem and all we could do for a month was bow in deep reverence and worship as the presence of God was felt in our midst. We worked during the day, but spent many nights worshipping the Lord, experiencing God's glory profoundly, in a real movement of the Spirit, in ways that have marked me forever.

By that time in my life, I had developed a deep trust in the Lord and an insatiable thirst for His Word. I found myself poring over Scripture, especially in the early morning when the world was still. I would ponder and think about the preaching and teaching I had heard and comb through the Word of God, rereading important Scripture passages, and tucking them into my heart.

Occasionally, I would find a passage that I could not understand, and I would open my trusty "Crudens Concordance" or one of the many Bible commentaries I had on hand. One time, I was pondering a question and finally went to my pastor to ask him, "How did Jesus remain sinless if He was born of a human, mortal woman who was born after the Fall and in sin?"

He listened intently, sitting behind his large desk, blinking slowly through his glasses, and finally said, "I have to think on that, and I'll get back to you." But he was busy, and he never did.

The ministry in Virginia was "interdenominational," open to Christians of different denominations. I began to meet Catholics who would come and visit the campground and sometimes stay at the cabins. I also began to meet Catholics in my travels to other countries on missions, especially priests and nuns. But

I could not understand why they were Catholic. They seemed to believe in Jesus; many were "Spirit-filled," read the Bible, and loved God, so I could not figure out why they would remain in the Catholic Church!

During one of my very first foreign mission trips in Manila, in the Philippines, our team was conducting meetings in a soccer stadium. The meetings were televised every night of the crusade, and the stadium itself was packed night after night. There were miraculous healings. On the last night of the meeting, the television manager came up to my pastor and offered him three more days of television and use of the stadium, free of charge. My pastor didn't hesitate! I was his assistant, so I dutifully reminded him that half our team was leaving in the morning for meetings somewhere else. He thought about that for a moment and said, "Go get some volunteers!"

A woman who had been standing, seeking prayer, piped up and said, "Can I bring some friends from my church? We'll help!" I looked back at my pastor and he said, "Bring them all!"

The next day, after saying goodbye to half of our team, we were back at the stadium to prepare for another night, and the volunteers began to gather. And then I saw this lady from the night before walking across the grass toward us with a group of priests and nuns following her! I knew this was not okay and that it was not going to work! After all, I'd been trained on how to minister to and *win* Catholics to Christ!

I looked at my pastor to see what he would do. He didn't even hesitate but practically ran to them to shake their hands and thank them for helping! I found this confusing. I wondered, *Doesn't he know what they believe?*

Later, especially in Europe and the United States, we found it easy to witness to and pray for Catholics who would end up in our churches. I later realized that these were mostly lapsed, even "cultural," Catholics. Many had not been practicing their faith for a long time, if ever.

One year, we were in Hong Kong for Christmas, after preaching in many countries and traveling since September. China had just begun to open up and allow outsiders visas into their country. We had been praying for China for years and were so happy to be able to enter the country, meeting with people from the underground churches and bringing them Bibles in Chinese. Our friends and fellow teammates who had been traveling throughout Southeast Asia arrived, and it was a great reunion as we shared experiences and "glory stories," reveling in the fruits of our endeavors.

While we were in Hong Kong, on Christmas Eve I had a dream that I was at home in Virginia, having a baby during a snowstorm. After many years of married life and missionary life, my husband and I still did not have children. I had prayed many times, and God would speak to my heart, telling me that He heard me and that He would answer with children in His time. And every Mother's Day, I would sit in silence with empty arms.

After this dream, when we were back in the United States, I went to the doctor, expecting some hopeful news, because of that dream! But, instead, he told me that it looked like I was never going to have children. I was completely devastated. Previously I'd been in to see him, and I had always remained optimistic, but now hope and all optimism were destroyed. I returned home upset and conflicted. "But, God . . . You said . . ."

When I got home, I found out that the ministry director had announced that there was going to be a special meeting that night, with a special guest speaker from Ireland. I did not want to go. My mind was made up; I wanted to stay home. But then I dragged myself up and, with a bruised heart, left my little missionary cottage and went into the meeting, only to be immediately annoyed.

There appeared to be a Catholic priest in the speaker's seat!

I was not in the mood for this. Again I thought, *Don't they know what these people believe?* I stayed in the back entryway, my arms crossed. Soon, after a time of singing praise and songs of worship, our speaker, Fr. Sandy Thompson from Ireland, a friend of Ruth in Jerusalem, was introduced.

As he took the podium, I busied myself getting ready to leave, and immediately the priest said, "There's someone here who's been told they will never have a child. God told me to pray for you." And then he just waited.

What? I had not yet told one person what the doctor had told me that day. I stuck my head in the room and looked around to see who else was there that could not have children. The priest just stood there, patiently, until he said it again. "There's someone here who's been told they will never have a child. God told me to pray for you."

My friend, who was in the back with me, who knew I'd been praying for a baby, came up to me and elbowed me in the ribs and whispered, "That's *you*!" But there was no way in the world I was going to let that Catholic priest near me, much less pray for me. And then Fr. Sandy had another inspiration of the Holy Spirit and mentioned other things to pray for and began to pray for other people. I was relieved and yet … And then he said it again, "There's someone here …"

My heart was pounding, and I had tears in my eyes. I was so conflicted. He was *Catholic*. And I had been taught all about Catholics and had earned a certificate after learning how to evangelize them.

And yet, I wanted a baby so very badly.

Slowly I walked to the front, halfway hoping someone else would say *they* were the one needing that prayer. The priest smiled and instructed Viola, one of the ladies near the front, to put her hands on my abdomen. And then he began to pray, basically for everything that the doctor had told me that very day. The Holy Spirit was showing the priest what I needed!

Later, I listened to his message as he spoke, mostly to be polite after he had prayed so ardently for me. And then I fled to my little home. I was exhausted, and this was so confusing.

One year later, Fr. Sandy Thompson was back. And again, we had a special meeting with him as the guest speaker. But this time, I ran up to him with tears in my eyes, asking him for a blessing and handing him my newborn daughter, Sarah. And yes, she was born at home, during a snowstorm! Exactly as in my dream. Fr. Sandy came back several times, and each time, I brought him my daughter, and then a few years later, my son, to receive a blessing from him.

While I was ecstatic at becoming a mother, I was also finally coming to terms with the fact that maybe Catholics could be Christians, and maybe my well-intentioned friends, early teachers, and mentors had gotten something not quite right when it came to the Catholic Church. But I wondered how it could be true.

4
Discoveries

The feeling remains that God is on the journey, too.

— St. Teresa of Avila

†

The years passed, and soon we had three beautiful miracle children, each one a unique gift from the Lord! We were busy with the day-in and day-out of our growing family and all the different aspects of full-time ministry.

The Iron Curtain had come down, and every month there were teams leaving for Eastern Europe, Russia, China, and the rest of the world to preach the gospel. It was a time when it seemed anything was possible, and it was! God was moving in beautiful ways, and untold millions were hearing the gospel and were coming to Christ, receiving healing and restoration! I even took my middle daughter, Stephanie, on her first mission to Eastern Europe when she was only six months old.

Then in the early '90s our family was sent out to start a church and to minister in Washington and later in the Dakotas, where our last child, Danielle, would be born. But soon our director called us back to Virginia to help with the growth and expansion in ministry there.

Revival was happening and the crowds were increasing, and Kerry and I, now with four kids, were busier than ever. And then, in December 1996, my friend and mentor Rev. Wallace Heflin, or "Brother Heflin" as we called him, unexpectedly and suddenly died. We were heartbroken. He was more than a mentor or a pastor, but was like a father to us. We didn't realize it then, but his death changed everything. After his funeral in Richmond, which was attended by thousands of people from all over the world whom he had helped launch into ministry, his sister, Ruth, from the ministry in Jerusalem, came to be the new director of our community.

One day, during the annual summer camp meeting, Ruth asked me if I would drive a visiting priest from London, England, to St. Ann's in town in the morning. I agreed and, after getting my kids into Sunday school, we headed out and had a lovely little chat as we drove the short distance to the beautiful and historic St. Ann's Catholic Church. When we arrived, I drove around the back to let him get out. I asked when I should pick him up. He seemed surprised and said, "Well, you're coming in, aren't you?"

I actually had no intention of going in. "Could I?" I asked, while in my heart I thought, *Should I?*

He waited while I parked the car, and we walked in together through a back door. He led me to a seat in the second row and then disappeared. We were there quite early, and I sat there, gaping at the beauty of that historic old church. There were the statues I had always been warned about. "Idols," I said to myself. But they didn't seem like idols, situated in the church glittering with gold and beautiful stained-glass windows depicting religious scenes from the Bible.

The walls were covered in Scripture! This literally stunned me as I had been told that Catholics didn't read the Bible! I didn't know what I was expecting, but this was not it! My priest friend was the guest homilist, and he gave a beautiful, Christ-centered message. I stumbled my way forward during Communion, and crossing my arms as instructed, received a blessing.

By the late '90s, I was traveling a lot for meetings in the United States and had begun speaking more and more often. In the early days, I had been part of teams, helping, learning, praying, leading the singing, or recording for our radio and TV shows. Gradually, I had become one of the featured speakers, and was often studying Scripture to prepare for conferences or meetings. Also, about this time, Kerry and I began attending seminars and conferences in Tulsa and became associates with AFCM, Association of Faith Churches and Ministries, where we were both ordained.

Renewal or revival was in the air in places like Pensacola and Toronto; thousands of people were returning to Christ, and the Holy Spirit was transforming people's lives. More and more people began to visit our little missionary headquarters from all over the world. On any given day we'd have visitors from India, Africa, Asia, Europe, Brazil, and all over America. Some stayed in hotels in town, many stayed in one of the motel-style buildings and dormitories on the grounds. Some brought trailers or tents and camped! It was a busy, wondrous time as we sang and prayed and saw the Lord move in our midst, as hearts were being drawn closer to Him.

That particular year, there were a lot of Catholics visiting from France and some from New York. The Holy Spirit had inspired me to write a little song, a chorus really, which the folks from France translated and began singing at every meeting in French.

Face to face,
In your glory.
Face to face,
In this place.
I will worship You forever,
As we stand,
Face to face.

It was fun, but they were Catholic, and even after visiting St. Ann's, I was frustrated that they were all remaining Catholic and going to Mass in town all the time.

Fr. Owen Lally from Jamaica, New York, and Sr. Yvonne were there again that year. Fr. Owen would sit near where I was seated with four kids, and one day he gave me a beautiful cross, which I later found out was a Benedictine cross. With it, he included a lovely letter ending with, "I am praying for you." I have both the cross and the letter to this day. And yet, I still could not understand at that time why he remained Catholic; clearly, he was full of faith in God and filled with the Holy Spirit!

Was it really possible that someone could be both Catholic and truly Christian? It was only much later that I realized, God had brought Fr. Owen into my life to challenge me about what it means to be a follower of Jesus.

†

One morning I finished speaking from the main stage on a series I was doing on the Song of Solomon, and a man came up to me and offered to lend me a book. His name was Bill Wolner and he had come with his wife Cheryl to volunteer at the camp for the summer. He was one of those Catholics from New York, and he was saying something about my message reminding him of someone, and could he lend me this book. *What? I didn't have time for this.*

However, being a longtime part of the ministry team, plus a speaker, I wanted to put my best foot forward, and decided to accept his offer graciously. That night he brought the book he had mentioned and gave it to me as I headed home from the evening meeting. It remained next to my bed, unopened for a couple of days.

Finally, Bill and Cheryl were getting ready to leave, and Bill asked if he could have his book back. So, the night before they were leaving, I thought I should at least take a look at it. I read the front cover with suspicion. The slim forty-day devotional was called *Majestic Is Your Name*. It was based on the writings of a woman I'd never heard of, but I recognized the editor, a columnist for *Charisma* magazine, and saw that it was published by Bethany House Publishers. So I turned the book over and read the back cover, then opened to the table of contents. I thought, *Wow. The chapter headings are interesting. I should read a paragraph or two.* So I did. And then I read a page. And then a chapter. Then I read this:[2]

> If you want to make great advances in prayer . . . if you want to walk the "high road" in spirit and reach the chambers of the King, then you must *remember* this: the truest, deepest prayer, that is, spiritual communion with God, does not consist in how much we know of doctrines or spiritual truth. True prayer consists in how much we are set free to love. (St. Teresa of Avila, *The Interior Castle*)

I was hooked, and I could not put the book down. Before I knew it, I had read the entire thing. And I was shocked. We thought our ministry was "cutting edge"! We thought our worship was new and fresh! That our love of the Beloved was a recent revelation!! But this book had been written five hundred years ago . . . by a Catholic nun! The meaning in her words was so current. I had never heard of St. Teresa of Avila, but I became an ardent follower that night.

In the morning as I handed Bill his book, I said, "Do you have any more of these kind of books?" He chuckled and gave me some ideas, but first I ordered my own copy of *Majestic Is Your Name*.

[2] *Majestic Is Your Name: A 40-Day Journey in the Company of Teresa of Avila*, ed. David Hazard (Minneapolis: Bethany, 1993), 149–150.

This time I went through slowly. Savoring each word. I would underline and circle what pierced my heart, and cross out with bold X's what sounded "too Catholic." Later, I wondered about Bill's offer to "lend" me the book instead of giving it to me, and I came to the conclusion that if he had merely "given" it, without needing it back, I may never have opened it!

The writings of Teresa of Avila were feeding me. It was like finding a pure fountain in a desert when I didn't realize how thirsty I was. I reveled in the way she wrote of our Lord and the spiritual life. I looked her up and read every book I could find about her! I wanted to read all of her writings. As I read biographies about her, I found out she was a "Doctor of the Church," and that there were others! So I went on to read the writings of all the Doctors of the Church that I could get my hands on and discovered the early Church Fathers' writings and stories along the way. This went on for a couple of years.

As I was voraciously reading my new books and discovering a part of Church history that I knew nothing about, someone gave me a CD series by a man named Ralph Martin, who was teaching about St. Teresa of Avila and the Doctors of the Church. I had never heard of Ralph Martin or Renewal Ministries, but the teaching was fantastic. I listened to the CDs over and over and waited for the next installment in the series to come out with anticipation that surprised me!

Up until now, I had only been reading. But in the recordings, I was listening to the voice of a Catholic man teaching on the Doctors of the Church with clarity and passion. I listened to some of those CDs several times and was intrigued that this biblical, beautiful teaching was coming from a Roman Catholic!

I was finding there was not much in what he said that this non-Catholic could disagree with!

Ralph kept mentioning a letter called *Novo Millennio Inuente* by Pope John Paul II. I sent for a copy, and read:

> The great mystical tradition of the Church ... has much to say in this regard. It shows how prayer can progress, as a genuine dialogue of love, to the point of rendering the person wholly possessed by the divine Beloved, vibrating at the Spirit's touch, resting filially within the Father's heart. This is the lived experience of Christ's promise: "He who loves me will be loved by my Father, and I will love him and manifest myself to him" (Jn 14:21). It is a journey totally sustained by grace.
>
> Yes, dear brothers and sisters, our Christian communities must become genuine "schools" of prayer, where the meeting with Christ is expressed not just in imploring help but also in thanksgiving, praise, adoration, contemplation, listening with ardent devotion until the heart truly "falls in love." (*Novo Millennio Inuente* 33)

How could I have ever thought that the pope was not a Christian? The words of the future St. John Paul the Great spoke to me so deeply! I ended up ordering a case of the booklets and giving them to everyone I knew. "Look what God is doing for the Catholics!!" It was really, "Look what God is doing in me!!"

Ruth, our new director, noted my sudden enthusiasm for Pope John Paul II and St. Teresa of Avila and called me into her office, asking me to attend a Catholic conference in Pennsylvania that she had been invited to, as her representative. I was happy for the opportunity! I was reading about Catholics and had so many questions about Pope John Paul II, St. Teresa, and my new discoveries, St. John of the Cross and St. Bernard of Clairvaux!

Yet I was also apprehensive. I knew from what I learned as a young Christian that, although the writings of these particular Catholics seemed Christ-centered, the Catholic Church's practices and beliefs had gone off the rails. So, I made up my mind that I would go and decided that when anything really "Catholic" started to happen, I could just excuse myself.

The convening priest found a lovely couple for me to stay with, and I enjoyed the people and the talks and messages that were shared, although I mostly sat in the back during the conference, which took place in a beautiful church outside of Philadelphia. I was invited to dinner with some of the priests who seemed eager to learn who I was and what I was doing there. I enthusiastically told them about "discovering" Teresa of Avila and that I was making my way through the writings of the early Church Fathers, as well as the Doctors of the Church. They smiled and said they would pray for me.

Later that day, the priest from Boston came to me, his eyes twinkling, and asked me to hold out my hand. When I did, he laid a small gold case with a glass lid that he said contained a relic of St. Teresa of Avila! I was so touched that he would give this to me, but I wasn't quite sure what a relic was! I asked the priest, and he explained to me that a relic is a physical object, often a part of a saint's body or an object they personally owned, and is a tangible connection to the saint whose life inspires our devotion to the Lord and who can intercede on our behalf. I have to admit at being more than a little shocked and unsure about this.

But then I thought of the story of Elisha in 2 Kings 13:21, where, during a time of war, a dead man's body was thrown into the prophet Elisha's tomb and touched his bones, and the man came back to life. The power of God was still present in the body of Elisha, even after his death. So, I was able to make that connection, although I found it strange, macabre even, and yet fascinating. When I got home, I wanted to know exactly what this meant and went online searching for answers. Still, I thought it was a generous, loving gift, one that became only more meaningful as time went on, and I kept learning. Today it is one of my most treasured possessions.

On the last day of the conference, it was announced that there would be some kind of procession. I had avoided Mass and only looked at the church statues from a distance, as I kept asking the Lord to protect me from anything that was not from Him while I was in the building. This procession sounded like something I should definitely avoid.

The music started and I moved out of the sanctuary into the back hallway where I could still enjoy the music. I loved the presence of the Lord. I still do. I am home in His presence, and I live to worship Him. I closed my eyes and focused on God, softly singing along with the musicians.

Suddenly, the atmosphere changed. I could feel Him. Jesus was there in front of me. Waves of His presence began to wash over me. Tears came to my eyes, and I began to bow deeply as wave after wave of His love and life and goodness kept washing over me and filling me. I bowed again, and as I rose, I opened my eyes. The priest visiting from Omaha was standing right in front of me, holding a gold pole with what looked like a large golden starburst on the end. In the center of the starburst was a glass case with something white in it. I did not know what it was.

What I *did* know was that Jesus Himself was in front of me in that moment! I bowed again and worshipped my Lord and my

God! As the priest moved on, I remained in the back, watching the eucharistic procession continue to move through the church, not yet knowing what a monstrance was, not comprehending the phrase "Real Presence," and without a full understanding of the Eucharist. All I knew was that Jesus had actually been with me in the back of that Catholic church.

I went home immediately after saying goodbye to my new friends, pondering what it all meant, as I kept asking myself, "What do I do with *that*?"

5

I Trust You, Lord

Our glory is hidden in our pain, if we allow God to bring the gift of Himself in our experience of it.

— Henri Nouwen

†

I went back home and told Kerry all about my experience and showed him the relic of St. Teresa of Avila. He was very neutral about it all. He did not discourage me or encourage me and thought it was "interesting."

I was wanting a little more feedback and help than that. Although I treasured the relic that was given to me, and the amazing experience of sensing the presence of Jesus in the back of that Catholic church, I was concerned that maybe I was reading too many Catholic books. A ferocious fear of being deceived, of accepting idol worship and other terrible things, reared its head.

I knew Jesus had been in that church in Pennsylvania and that I had truly experienced His presence in a profound way. I also knew that those people loved God, but what about all the other stuff? And while I was in awe that I now had a real relic of my favorite saint, Teresa of Avila, in my possession, what about praying to saints and worshipping Mary, and Catholics being forbidden to read the Bible? What about the Antichrist? I had been trained so carefully, the list of objections I had to the Church was a mile long. Some of these people were obviously believers, but I was afraid.

A year had passed since the Wolners had invited me to St. Ann's for that Holy Thursday. The experience I'd had that night had stayed with me, and I remained amazed that Jesus would allow me to be with Him like that. I was still experiencing the sensation of His blood, mingled with water and sweat, on my foot. He was drawing me in to Himself. And I continued to wonder what it all meant.

After only a few years as director of the ministry, Ruth, too, died. A six-foot-two-inch old-fashioned Pentecostal woman, she possessed a natural charisma and ministered to many world leaders. At the time of her death, she had just completed her trip to North Korea, having visited every nation in the world. She had been and remains a big influence in my life. We mourned and grieved the loss and yet knew that God was holding all things in His Hands.

A new director was appointed, and we soon experienced a large turnover of staff. Change was in the air, and my husband Kerry began to sense that the American Church was in need of ministry and renewal, and he prayerfully decided to begin to focus on ministering in the United States, specifically the heartland.

In 2002 we packed up our belongings, said goodbye to our friends in Virginia, and moved our family to the upper Midwest of the United States. We got busy starting a church and pioneering ministries all through North and South Dakota, Minnesota, and Wisconsin, sharing the gospel anywhere the door was open, while still speaking across the country for conferences and revivals. We began to bring teams together, and over the course of several years we preached in prisons, at country clubs, churches, hotels, park band shells—all for the love of God and people. We also had meetings on Native American reservations in Minnesota, the Dakotas, and Wisconsin.

Initially, I was not sure about going to the Native American reservations, or the "rez" as the Native Americans called them. But God began to deal with my heart, and He asked me if I was willing. And I was. The tribal elders in Pine Ridge were the first to extend the invitation for us to come. We received permission to erect a large tent that could sit four hundred people, and team members came from as far away as England to participate as we came to love the people, to share the gospel with them, and to pray and watch God move in their lives. It was a fruitful time full of so many wonderful stories of what God did!

At the same time, people from overseas continued to ask us to come, and we started to train people for short-term missions. Soon I was taking our own teams all over the world.

And in the midst of it all, I continued to read. Many evenings, after everyone was asleep, when the house was dark and quiet, I would find myself online, reading the works of Clement of Rome, Ignatius of Antioch, Polycarp of Smyrna, and another early church documents. As I read Polycarp, I was stunned to realize that we had the writings from a disciple of St. John! It was a direct connection to the apostles. This filled me with reverence and awe. Somehow, in my circles, we liked to quote Calvin or John Knox or Martin Luther as "historic" sources. Reliable church history just didn't seem to go back any further than that!

I remember sitting in my home office, reading these earliest Christians, wondering why I had never known these names before, and being excited at the Christian message they contained.

About this time, my stepmom, Gayle, called to tell me that she and my father were coming out to visit us. I had been praying for my father ever since I had become a Christian. We had not been particularly close, especially after I had left to go to Virginia, but I had received a lot of healing in my heart through the power of forgiveness, and I was happy they were coming.

They arrived just a couple of days before Father's Day. A special guest speaker was scheduled to speak at our church for the Father's Day service, and that morning, I was surprised to find my dad and Gayle all dressed up for church! "Oh, Dad, don't feel like you *have* to come," I said.

"He doesn't," Gayle answered for him."He wants to come. We both do."

I chuckled to myself. Our special guest that morning was from South Africa and was very lively. After all these years, *this* is the service my dad wants to come to?

When the service began, my dad and Gayle sat in the first row! I was watching from the keyboard, smiling at them. Later, when the visiting speaker was ending his sermon, he invited persons to come forward who wanted to receive Jesus as their Lord and Savior, and I saw my dad, who had once proclaimed that he didn't believe in organized religion, come forward. It was a miracle, and even though I was seeing it, I could hardly believe that it was happening. I had prayed, forgiven, and prayed some more. And now my dad was becoming a Christian at our church, on Father's Day!

One day, around midmorning, I was home cleaning up the house and getting ready for church that night. My oldest child was married and living in town, and the rest of my children were at school, with one at the local college. My husband had been out of town for meetings and had stopped late at night and checked into a motel in South Dakota on the way home. I was expecting him at any moment.

There was a knock at the front door, and I was surprised to see a policeman and another gentleman on the front steps. They asked if they could come in, and once we got to the living room, they asked my name, and then they told me that Kerry, my husband, had died.

In that moment, my entire world turned upside down. I kept making them repeat what they said, as I couldn't seem to take it in. It was hard to believe. He had checked into the hotel and gone to bed, but he never awoke from his sleep. They had been told it looked like a catastrophic stroke. Because he was from out of state, and had died alone at the motel, his body would be released only after an MIA (minimally invasive autopsy).

The rest is a blur. They kept talking, giving me advice, and asking me which funeral home I wanted his body sent to when it was released. It was all so sudden. It was unbelievable. It was too much.

Finally, they left, and still reeling and in a daze, I began to make phone calls. Then, I had to tell my children. This remains the most difficult thing I have ever had to do in my entire life, and it brings tears to my eyes even now. I picked up the kids from school and told the two older kids to meet us at the house. The kids were anticipating the nightly after-dinner game with Dad after the dinner dishes were done. It was a terrible blow. He had not been himself for quite a while, and looking back, there seemed to be signs that something was off, but at the time we had been completely unaware of the shocking catastrophe just around the corner.

The days, weeks, months, and even years that followed were unbelievably hard. It was all a blur, from the first days after the officer came to my home to the planning of the funeral and its aftermath. In the weeks that followed, after all the family and helpers and friends were gone, the intense shock turned into a growing ache. In prayer, I would say to the Lord, "I never knew anyone could hurt like this," and I would think of all those whom

I knew who had been through terrible ordeals and loss, and I would pray for them.

There were more than a few days I didn't want to leave my room, except to take the kids to school. I didn't get out of my pajamas but would just throw a coat on and go. Sorrow, anger, regret, and hurt engulfed me as I witnessed the heartbreak of my children. I would stare at the wall in my room and say, "Lord, is *this* how you answer my prayers?"

Then, just as I felt I was drowning in my grief, God sent a longtime friend, the late Rev. John (Jack) Chappell. Looking back, I believe Brother Chappell literally saved my life, as he would not allow me to sink into total despair. He and his wife Pattie—gifted speakers and missionaries who had ministered all over the world—were like spiritual parents to me. He helped me begin to thank God in *all* things and not judge God by how I felt, but find rest and truth in the Word of God.

And while I knew theologically that God was with us and had encountered His love in so many ways, I was now learning to lean into the Lord in a way I never had before. And even though I couldn't help but ask "why" in my heart, I had to keep surrendering the questions to God and trust Him even when I could not understand Him. I learned to be still and not panic when I didn't know the way forward or out of the dark.

I would literally breathe, "I trust You, Lord," throughout the day, choosing to trust Him, when I didn't feel like trusting, or even want to. Eventually I sat at my piano again, and was able, with a breaking voice, to sing the old hymn "It Is Well with My Soul" and make it my prayer.

When peace, like a river attendeth my way,
When sorrows like sea billows roll.

Whatever my lot, Thou hast taught me to say,
It is well, it is well with my soul.
It is well with my soul, it is well, it is well with my soul.

Though Satan should buffet, though trials should come,
Let this blest assurance control,
That Christ hath regarded my helpless estate,
And hath shed His own blood for my soul.
It is well with my soul, it is well, it is well with my soul.

For me, be it Christ, be it Christ hence to live:
If Jordan above me shall roll,
No pang shall be mine, for in death as in life,
Thou wilt whisper Thy peace to my soul.
It is well with my soul, it is well, it is well with my soul.[3]

Amazingly, almost imperceptibly, as I kept choosing to surrender what I could not make sense of and to trust God's hand in our lives, and with a lot of love and support from our friends, I began to see daybreak. God was sheltering me in His love in a way I had never experienced before.

It was at this time that I began focusing on the writings of another saint and Doctor of the Church, St. John of the Cross, whom I was delighted to find was a close companion of St. Teresa of Avila. His writings brought such meaning to me and light in the darkness. Later, looking back, I can see that my heavy loss became the means by which I was brought even closer to the Heart of my Beloved Lord.

[3] "It Is Well with My Soul," by Horatio G. Spafford (1876), is in the public domain.

6

Revelations

I will give you the treasures of darkness and the hoards in secret places, that you may know that it is I, the LORD . . . who calls you by name.

— Isaiah 45:3

†

Six months later, I slowly resumed ministering and speaking. A year later, I sold my little house on the James River and moved to "the Cities" with Danielle, my youngest. Danielle was still in high school, while the rest were at college or with their young families. I was still deeply feeling our loss, but I felt it was time to move forward. I rented a house and began learning to navigate life on my own.

I was speaking all around Minneapolis and had begun to travel again, and the missions and mentoring were fruitful. And yet, it was at this time that I would find myself visiting Catholic churches when I had a few moments to spare. I remember spending a lot of time at the beautiful Cathedral of St. Paul (in St. Paul), thinking of my experience at St. Ann's and at the church outside of Philadelphia. I began to revisit my Catholic books, reading and rereading the early Church Fathers late into the night. They spoke so authoritatively about Jesus, and lived lives totally consecrated to God; their teachings and writings often seemed to overflow with the Holy Spirit!

I had been teaching and preaching about the "presentness" of the Kingdom of God, the immediacy of the Kingdom, that God was *with* us, and I found this same message resonating throughout the history of the Roman Catholic Church. The martyrs, early Church Fathers and Mothers, and saints were Christians who had chosen to walk *with* God, not just for Him. And God showed up everywhere they went!

I'm not sure exactly how long I had been reading from the treasury of the early church when I was gripped with a profound revelation: *the Roman Catholic Church is Pentecostal!* Not "practicing Pentecostalism," but vibrant with the life of the Holy Spirit, the third Person of the Trinity. I discovered that the Catholic Church even has a feast dedicated to the Holy Spirit, "the feast of Pentecost," or "Pentecost Sunday"!

Neither could it be argued that the Catholic Church was cessationist (a belief that the Holy Spirit ceased working after the age of the apostles). The lives of the saints were full of the miraculous, supernatural, glorious power of God, confirming what they were teaching and preaching. As the *Catechism of the Catholic Church* teaches:

> Whether extraordinary or simple and humble, charisms are graces of the Holy Spirit which directly or indirectly benefit the Church, ordered as they are to her building up, to the good of men, and to the needs of the world. Charisms are to be accepted with gratitude by the person who receives them and by all members of the Church as well. They are a wonderfully rich grace for the apostolic vitality and for the holiness of the entire Body of Christ, provided they really are genuine gifts of the Holy Spirit and are used in full conformity with authentic promptings of this same Spirit, that is, in keeping with charity, the true measure of all charisms. (CCC 799–800)

The early church was the Catholic Church. Never, since the Church was founded, had God been merely a religious theory or philosophy to the apostles or their successors. His life and love had become real to them through the person of Jesus, Who taught them of the Father (John 10:30) and promised to send them the Holy Spirit, the Paraclete (John 14:25–26). For Jesus' first followers, the love of God was the reason the universe and everything in it was formed. They were able to lay down their lives for the sake of Jesus, because they knew that to walk with God was to possess everything, and that without God, the world had nothing for them.

Since that time, the Church has literally been immersed in the love of God, the whole life of the Trinity, teaching the faithful to live and give witness expressing that life, often with extraordinary signs accompanying them.

From the beginning, the world has turned to Christ not because of rules or oppressive practices but because of the love of God that was revealed through the Spirit-led, Spirit-filled lives of His witnesses, along with the great wisdom and powerful preaching of so many. The testimony was their history.

Despite these discoveries, there were still so many Catholic things—so many modern beliefs and practices I had heard about—that I could not reconcile with the basic tenets of Christianity as I had understood them from Scripture. So I got online, typing in my questions:

- † Why do Catholics worship Mary?
- † Why pray the Rosary?
- † Why do Catholics pray to saints instead of Jesus?
- † What is papal infallibility?

Finally, one day when I was searching, I found the *Coming Home Network*, a Catholic apostolate that was run by Marcus Grodi and other former Protestant ministers who had become Catholic and were endeavoring to answer the questions of their Protestant brothers and sisters in ministry about the Church of Rome.

I was intrigued. Finally, I could ask questions anonymously and even argue without hurting anyone's feelings! I signed up and began to post my questions, objections, and concerns. They seemed to understand my hesitancy and anticipate my questions! The resident theologian would post the answers to my queries for anyone to see, but I was known only by my user name. I felt safe. This was great!

And so I began asking questions, getting answers, checking those answers against other sources, backing off, and then asking more questions.

One day, Jim Anderson at the *Coming Home Network* contacted me and asked if he could send some books. Books? Yes please! I was expecting two, but he sent a whole box of them! I was especially intrigued by the books by the former Evangelical professor Thomas Howard. I read all the books Jim sent and continued to ask my questions on what the Church actually teaches. Then I would back off, sometimes for months at a time. While I found many of their answers reassuring, there was still one subject that gave me pause: Mary.

It was around this time that my reading of church history had brought me from the early church to the Reformation era. There was one book in particular—I cannot remember the name or the author, and I don't have it anymore because I shared those books with everyone I knew—that opened my eyes to the great historic "divide" in the Church. When I finished the little book, I remember sitting back in my office chair and pondering what it all meant.

I could certainly see that the original, violent outbreak of Protestantism morphed into nationalism, and not everyone's motives were about the Kingdom of God. Instead of a true reformation, there had been a conflagration and lasting separation, on both sides, that left a stain on Christianity. Instead of remaining inside the Church and working for reform, as St. Francis of Assisi did, the desire of almost all Protestants was to separate from the Church, no matter the cost, and be their own church. In fact, after John Calvin made Geneva his headquarters, it was referred to as the "New Rome." All this meant that the "other" side had to be vilified, by all parties.

I knew that in that era the Catholic Church was in need of reform, but I had *never* studied the movement to reform the Catholic Church from within that became the life's work of so many of my favorite saint—including St. Teresa of Avila and St. John of the Cross. Now, as I began to study, I would sit back and wonder, *What do you do when you realize you may be on the wrong side of a fight?* What do you do when you realize someone handed on to you a prejudice, even to the point of slander, against other Christians?

I thought of all the Protestant church splits that I had personally witnessed. Christians kept on dividing, even to this day. And I knew that only one entity in all of creation benefited from it. El Diablo, the Slanderer, the Divider. There was a lot to ponder.

I noticed one day when I was speaking at a church in Grand Forks, North Dakota, that an illustration from St. John of the Cross had made its way into my message.

> The fire of love that will afterward unite with the soul and bring it glory is the same fire which begins to assail it in order to cleanse and purify.... Think of the way fire

> penetrates a log, as the flame begins to burn away the outer imperfections, stripping the log of scars and roughness. As its heat mounts, the fire penetrates into the log itself, until wood and flame are one. Just so, fire transforms wood into fire. (St. John of the Cross, *Dark Night of the Soul*)

On the way home, I began to wonder if I was reading too many Catholic books.

It had been three years since Kerry had died, and the Holy Spirit spoke to my heart and said that it was time for a sabbatical. I wrestled with it and then said yes. I had thirteen months of meetings on the calendar; however, as I contacted the pastors and ministry partners, they overwhelmingly supported the sabbatical, and everything was rescheduled. I organized some time to seek God, study, and rest.

On the first day of my official sabbatical, my mother called and told me she had been diagnosed with fourth-stage non-Hodgkins lymphoma, and that the outlook was not good. I told her I was on my way.

Years earlier, I had received a lot of inner healing through prayer ministry, learning the power of forgiveness. I received training in healing the whole person and spent years praying and ministering to pastors and laypeople, watching God set them free from their woundedness and offenses. I had forgiven both my parents, and our relationships had been healed. God had worked in my heart until I was able to love them both freely and deeply.

So I packed my bags and gathered my books from the *Coming Home Network* and flew to Washington state to be with my mother. I had people all over the country praying for her. We practiced laughter therapy to get the endorphins working, meaning I told her a lot of jokes to make her laugh, and we watched a lot of her favorite movies, especially anything with Lucille Ball.

One day, I was sitting with my mom while she was getting treated at the hospital. I was reading when she grew bored with the television, and she asked me to read to her. There was no way I was going to tell my mother, whom I had been praying for all these years, that her missionary daughter was reading Catholic books! But she kept asking me what I was reading, and finally I told her, "They're Catholic! I'm reading Catholic books!" And I went on to confess to her that I was visiting and praying in Catholic churches and cathedrals, and that I didn't know what it was, but there was just something there in those churches that was drawing me!

She looked up at me with her big blue eyes and said matter-of-factly, "Well, you know you were baptized Catholic!"

What? No! I did not know this! I had no idea I'd even been to a Catholic church as a child, much less that I'd been baptized Catholic. I was actually thrilled!

For the next hour, while we were waiting for the doctor, we talked about her childhood, and the faith she had as a child. She told me that I had been baptized at St. Francis Xavier Catholic Church in St. Louis, Missouri, when I was nine months old, at the urging of her grandmother, Madeleine. It was the same grandmother Madeleine who urged that my mom be baptized when *she* was a baby. I was stunned! Later, I called St. Francis Xavier in St. Louis to verify my baptism there, and within weeks had my baptismal certificate!

At the time, I didn't even believe in infant baptism. But I'd not forgotten The Man in the Sky and that, when I came to Christ and became a believer, I realized "The Man" was Jesus! But I never understood *why* He was with me. I didn't think I had anyone praying for me. Why did I love Him so? Now, I knew! When my mother said I'd been baptized, I suddenly understood that, while I did not know I was in covenant with God through the Sacrament of Baptism, God *never forgot* that He was in covenant with me! It was Amazing Grace—grace I didn't even ask for. God freely bestowed it upon me!

Later, back at her house, my mother began to open up and talk about her childhood and the panic attack she'd recently had before I arrived, while having her first PET scan. As she was belted down and slid into the tube, she had flashbacks of being three years old, living in a preschool boarding school in Hollywood, California, where she would be locked into her crib at night and left alone, crying for her mother. I never knew any of this, as my mom had never talked about her childhood much. But, oh, my heart went out to her.

We talked a long while about her life, about her mother, who was a model and a single mother after divorcing her father, captain of a shipping vessel. We talked about the different boarding schools she had attended, all Catholic, and her grandmother in St. Louis with whom she lived when she was not in a boarding school, and her Catholic grandmother in California who used to pray for her.

And then she told me that in junior high school, there was a time she seriously considered becoming a nun! I asked her when she felt the safest in her life. And she said, "With the nuns."

The Holy Spirit was moving in our conversation, prompting me to tell her it was time to return to the God of her childhood. It was time to go back to that place where she knew God. Especially now as she was facing cancer, when she needed prayer and encouragement, this was the place to find refreshment. I gently encouraged her to go back to the Church, the Roman Catholic Church. And then we prayed.

I was with my mom for her last PET scan. No one could believe the results: all the cancer was gone, and she has now been cancer free for more than fifteen years!

When I returned home from being with my mother, I had a lot to think about. First of all, I was praising God that I had been able to pray with my mother, prayers of inner healing and freedom, prayers that the Lord would remind her of His great love for her. And at the same time, I could not believe I had just encouraged my mom to go back to the Roman Catholic Church.

But most of all, I could not get over the fact that I had been baptized when I was nine months old, and when I received the certificate in the mail, it was like finding a treasure.

7

Friends in Faith

Iron sharpens iron, and one man sharpens another.

— Proverbs 27:17

†

My sabbatical was ending, and I was gearing up to be on the road for meetings, as Danielle was now at college. Of course, the very first place that happened to be on my schedule was St. Louis, and I took the first opportunity I had to visit St. Francis Xavier Church, which is absolutely beautiful, the "college" church at the Jesuit college, Saint Louis University.

I stood by the baptismal font in wonder, looking around and trying to take it all in. A priest walked up to me and gruffly asked me what I was doing there. As I began to tell him that I was a Pentecostal missionary and evangelist who just found out I'd been baptized there, in that church, at that baptismal font, I got all teary eyed. He took my hand and gently asked where I'd been as a missionary and I began to tell him some of the places I'd been, and how I'd witnessed the Lord moving in the hearts and lives of so many people.

And then he told me, "You know, St. Francis Xavier is the patron saint of missionaries! You've come back to where it all began."

In fact, I did not know this. But it seemed to make sense, and on the inside, I thought, *Of course!*

He gave me a tour of the beautiful building, and then I returned to my hotel to focus on the meeting I would be speaking at that night for a prophetic church in the suburbs.

While in my hotel room, and throughout the meeting that night, I knew the Lord was calling me to start sharing my journey and what was happening in my heart, especially now that I found out I was baptized in the Roman Catholic Church as a child. Put simply, I needed to talk to someone about what was going on!

I prayed about it and soon I sensed the Lord leading me to call my friend Deborah Kendrick, whom I had known since "the early days," and who had been a longtime friend and ministry associate. I knew she would give me wise counsel. I was a little nervous when I called. A deeply gifted woman, I knew she would speak straight with me and not hold back.

After talking about our kids, it all came tumbling out. I told her about my deep attraction to all things Catholic and that I was reading everything about the Catholic Church I could get my hands on, that I had been reading about the saints and their writings for several years, that I was visiting Catholic churches, and that I was finding there was something there. Finally, I stopped and took a breath, and then held my breath, waiting for her to tell me I was out of my mind and to burn the books.

Instead, much to my astonishment, she said, "Me too!"

"What?" I couldn't believe it! "What do you mean?"

"Me too!" She said again, and she started to tell me *her* story! I was hardly able to believe what I was hearing! She had been speaking at meetings all over Europe and had spoken at ecumenical meetings alongside someone named Fr. Raniero Cantalamessa (now Cardinal Cantalamessa and preacher to the papal household), whom she considered a friend. She shared about meetings at Catholic churches and concluded by saying that "the Catholics of Europe were loving me into the Church."

We could not believe what we were telling each other and that we were both in the midst of such similar journeys! After a good two hours, with both of us sharing, I asked her, "What do we do now?"

"I don't know!" she said. We both had the same cautions, concerns, and most of all, deep desire not to offend God.

We began to speak regularly, to share what we were learning and to pray together. Debbie spent so much time in France that two of her daughters married Frenchmen. Her son-in-law, Benoit, was a former seminarian from Paris. He was living and raising his family in a multigenerational household with Debbie and her husband Bill in Virginia. Now I finally had someone I could question and even argue with in person! So, I visited my old hometown in Virginia to see Debbie and Bill and lay out all my objections and questions to Benoit.

This was really new territory for all of us: Debbie, her husband Bill who was also looking at the Church, and myself. I had known so many people who had left the Catholic Church, but I had never met anyone who had lived a missionary life like mine, lived to bring people to Jesus and trained others to do the same, who was Catholic. At this point, I was just trying to understand their beliefs.

I can still see it so clearly, sitting in their family room, surrounded by Bill's beautiful artwork. Bill (a fine artist), sitting in his chair, with a book in his hands, saying, "I love it. I thought the Catholic Church was all about so-called saints and rules for reaching God, but it's all about Jesus!"

I was overjoyed to be reunited with them all. But to hear this from Bill was amazing! I spent hours talking, peppering Benoit with questions, parrying and coming back at him with Scripture, and he always gently explained the Catholic position, until I would begrudgingly admit that I could see his point.

After a beautiful time of fellowship with the Kendricks and visiting my old home and the ministry in Virginia, I returned home. There was a lot to think about.

My team and I had just gotten that month's ministry newsletter out. In the last year, I had taken groups to Israel, had led teams to minister and share the gospel and pray with people in Peru and Turkey, and had spoken again in Malaysia.

A group was coming to my house that night for a prayer meeting, more training in receptivity to the gifts of the Holy Spirit, and mission training. I was just getting ready to turn off my computer, when the Holy Spirit whispered to me, "You're going to take a class."

A class? This will be great! Maybe I could audit a Catholic Church History class at one of the nearby Catholic universities! So, I began browsing on the internet. And every time I found a class that looked interesting, I could literally hear a "no" inside of me. It was like the buzzer on a game show when you gave the wrong answer. It was a very clear "no."

On and off, over the next week, I browsed around online, looking up classes and information. "Lord, if You really said I'm going to take a class, You're going to have to show me what it is." And I waited. I had learned a long time ago not to push God. You remain docile and open to what He has said, positioning your heart for His direction, and then when God opens the door, you're ready and in position to go through it.

I had pretty much quit looking, when I was online for something completely unrelated, and an ad banner floated across my screen. The Lord spoke to my heart, "That's your class!" But by then the ad banner was gone! It had floated across the screen, and now I couldn't find it!

I tried retracing my online steps, until finally the banner began crossing my screen again … there it is! I clicked it and was redirected to a page for the Harry J. Flynn Catechetical Institute in St. Paul (sometimes called "CI"). I didn't even recognize the word "catechetical." I thought it might mean "teaching." This was the class I was to take. A two-year study of the *Catechism of the Catholic Church.*

†

When I called the phone number on the website to get more information, a woman answered. I told her I was interested in attending the Institute, carefully avoiding the word "catechetical," as I wasn't sure how it was pronounced. She was very business-like as I gave my name, address, etc., until she asked which parish I belonged to. "Oh, I'm not Catholic," I blurted out.

"Sorry, you can't attend ... this is for Catholics."

I quickly launched into an explanation of why I simply *had* to attend, and she finally told me that there was someone else I needed to speak to, and she gave me a phone number.

I took a deep breath, then dialed the number she gave me. A woman named Kelly Wahlquist answered. I explained to Kelly that I wanted to attend "the Institute" even though I was not a Catholic, that I was a Protestant minister appreciating what I was finding in the Catholic Church, and that the Holy Spirit *told* me to take this class.[4]

Finally, Kelly said, "I think there's someone else you need to talk to about this. Give me your phone number and I will have him give you a call." I gave her my number, hung up, and left it all in God's Hands.

Within a couple of days, I received a call from an unknown caller. "I understand you want to attend the Harry J. Flynn

4 Kelly later told me that she had been at her mother-in-law's lake house, outside of Minneapolis, when I called. Usually they did not get cell phone reception, but that "somehow" my call went through.

Catechetical Institute, even though you aren't Catholic, and that you're an active Protestant minister."

"Yes," I confirmed, happy at last to know how to pronounce "catechetical."[5]

"Would you mind telling me why you would like to attend?"

Out tumbled my story of reading the Catholic saints, visiting cathedrals and chapels, and finding myself mysteriously drawn to this Church that I had been taught to avoid. My face was wet with tears by the time I was finished telling him "why."

"That's an interesting story," he said. "Let me tell you my story."

He began to tell me of his journey of being born into a Catholic family, later becoming an Evangelical, and then a pastor, and then about watching Pope John Paul II on television during World Youth Day in Denver, which made him hungry for the Church he had left behind. I knew that he understood a little of what I was experiencing, and he also understood my language and where I was coming from. His own story is well documented. His name was Jeff Cavins.

Jeff told me he would make sure it was okay with the archbishop if I attended, but he was pretty sure there would be no problem. Soon, I was all signed up!

The day came for our first assembly before classes began. My future classmates and I gathered at the St. Mary's Chapel at Saint Paul Seminary on the University of St. Thomas campus. I had come alone and did not know a single person there. I did not participate in the Mass but stood in the back and watched the proceedings, just happy to be there. Jeff Cavins was introduced and welcomed

[5] kat-i-ḲET-i-kuhl.

us all, and I watched as he and a few other instructors later knelt before the archbishop to offer their vows to faithfully represent the Church and teach the *Catechism of the Catholic Church.*

And so began two years of study. Classes were on Monday nights, beginning at the seminary in St. Paul. Our class was named the Class of Pope John Paul II. I remember walking into the lecture hall the very first night of class and surveying the room, seeing about 175 Catholic men and women seated with Bibles, copies of the *Catechism*, and notebooks, waiting for class to begin. My kind of tribe! I had to pinch myself.

I finally met Kelly in person, who would later go on to found WINE, or Women in the New Evangelization, an apostolate formed to encourage evangelization among Catholic women. Warm and friendly, she definitely helped me feel not so out of place.

Each week, we had a lecture on our assigned readings from the *Catechism*, followed by small group discussions, and I was immediately enthralled. I made up my mind, based on the response I'd gotten from my earlier inquiries on the phone when first calling about the Institute, that I would not tell anyone that I was not Catholic or that I was a full-time preacher and speaker who traveled a lot. I also discovered in my small group that, in many ways, I already knew more about the Church than many of those attending the Institute!

How well I remember those first weeks. The prologue and the very opening paragraphs of the *Catechism* were so moving, so filled with Beauty and Biblical Truth!

> God, infinitely perfect and blessed in himself, in a plan of sheer goodness freely created man to make him share in his own blessed life. For this reason, at every time and in

> every place, God draws close to man. He calls man to seek him, to know him, to love him with all his strength. He calls together all men, scattered and divided by sin, into the unity of his family, the Church. To accomplish this, when the fullness of time had come, God sent his Son as Redeemer and Savior. In his Son and through him, he invites men to become, in the Holy Spirit, his adopted children and thus heirs of his blessed life.

I no longer understood how I could have doubted that these were Christians. As I went further into the *Catechism*, I found Scripture everywhere. I was a little surprised by this, but delighted. And trust me when I tell you I looked up every footnote.

Who said Catholics didn't read the Bible? Okay! Maybe many don't, but they *can*.

As we continued through the lessons, especially in the later sections, I did find there were things that I had a problem with, and I would attend the corresponding lecture with my mind made up, saying to myself, "*This* is why the Church is 'off,' " only to find myself processing during the entire drive home, because all my objections were addressed by the lecturer, even before I could bring them up, and I could see the truth and amazing beauty in the Church's teaching. I especially appreciated how Deacon Michalak laid out his thoughts with such great clarity.

In the meantime, I was still a mother, and now a grandmother, and a missionary of Christ, as always, busy with ministry. I was on the road many weekends, teaching the gospel and praying with people, and then flying home. Many times during my time at the Catechetical Institute, I flew into the Minneapolis airport on Monday evening, picked up my car, and drove straight to my class.

My friend Debbie and I were still praying together and wondering what to do with what we were learning. But as much as my soul was touched by what I was discovering, I was wrestling with doubts.

You may find it hard to believe, but after all those years of reading Clement and Ignatius of Antioch and Polycarp, Bernard of Clairvaux, Teresa of Avila, Catherine of Siena, and others, I still had only a limited idea of what actually was going on during Mass. I visited a nearby parish during Holy Week and sat in the back, listening intently to every word.

During the Liturgy of the Eucharist, when we got to the part, "May the Lord accept the sacrifice at your hands," I thought, *Do they always say that? I don't remember hearing that before*. And my reaction in my thoughts went automatically to "there no longer remains a sacrifice for sins" (Heb. 10:26), and I would think, *And that's why I'm not Catholic*.

Then I looked a little deeper, and I found out that the Sacrifice of the Mass is our participation in Christ's *one*, eternal sacrifice.

One afternoon I visited the beautiful St. Paul Cathedral, praying in the back and walking around and admiring the beauty, and wondering at the significance of the altars and the many statues of saints. Tour groups would often come to the cathedral, and there were many tourists in the church that afternoon. I noticed in the foyer that there would be a Mass early that evening, so I decided to stay and attend, as I had been discovering so much about the Sacrifice of the Mass.

I found a seat in the middle section, behind the cluster of Catholics attending who were bunched up in the front on a weekday evening. Many of the tourists also came to find a seat near where I was. The Mass began and the tourists didn't know what to do, or how to do it. We only watched and tried to keep up with hand gestures (the sign of the cross), congregational responses, kneeling.

In vain I looked around for a program or some kind of guide to help me through the Mass. There was nothing. I looked toward the people in front of me and saw all the good Catholics concentrating. There was no help there! I looked at the tourists around me who were there for Mass. They were also glancing around for some kind of "help" regarding what was happening and what they were witnessing, and what could help them participate in some measure. Nothing. I was able to participate in the "Our Father," but during the sign of peace, we in the back were on our own. Now some of the tourists were getting up to leave.

All the Catholics lined up for Communion. I had seen this before and was somewhat familiar with the process. But no one seemed to notice us people in the back.

After Mass was over, I felt a little deflated. I was an evangelist. I loved to introduce people to Jesus! And I just witnessed, to borrow terminology from Jesus, a bunch of fish trying to jump into the boat with no one manning the nets. Why didn't anyone care that we were there? Why didn't anyone reach out to the tourists who had stayed? With so much truth, beauty, and goodness, and with the exhortation to "go, and declare the good news," why didn't anyone give us that good news?

Ah, okay, I'm learning so much about the Church. I have come to see that they are Christians after all. So much of what I had been taught earlier in my Christian walk concerning them was incorrect.... But, this, *this* is why I could never be Catholic.

8
The Evangelists

The surest sign that God is alive in you is joy.
The minute you walk outside of your church
on Sunday, you're in mission territory.

— Bishop Robert Barron

†

I decided to find out if there were any Catholic evangelists who worked to bring others to Christ. By now I was familiar with much of early church history and knew of the men and women who laid down their lives to preach the gospel with the power of the Holy Spirit. I was also familiar with the names of many saints, male and female, whom God had used to bring about renewal and refreshing in the Church, and to bring people personally to a living faith in Jesus.

But what about this generation? How can we say we love our neighbors and not want to share the freeing, amazing message of Jesus with them? And yet, in years of being a pastor, evangelist, and traveling missionary, I had met so many lapsed Catholics who claimed never to have heard the "Kerygma," the gospel message, in a clear way.

Again, I ended up doing an online search, finding sites about Catholic apologetics as well as a smattering of small Catholic groups exhorting on the need to evangelize and share the good news of the gospel, as Jesus commanded. I was delighted to come across a Catholic priest from Chicago who was, to borrow his term, "engaging the culture." I played his online videos of talks and presentations, and was especially taken by his videos about *the "new" atheists*. I was thrilled to find this Catholic evangelist, Fr. Robert Barron, engaging and evangelizing non-Catholics! I even started sending links of some of his messages to ministry friends of mine. “Look!” I would say. “A Catholic evangelist talking about Jesus!!” I became a regular “follower,” and later, when he was appointed auxiliary bishop in Southern California, I watched his ordination online. Since then, the scope and reach of his ministry has had explosive growth, and he has been one of those leading the way in teaching the Faith to both Catholics and culture.[6]

One night I was browsing online, looking for Catholic evangelists, and discovered a video of a Catholic woman giving an interview. She was speaking about how she, a lifelong Catholic, was also a convert! She said that she woke up every morning full of her own agenda and had to continually be converted. She had to remind herself that she was a disciple of Jesus. That was Dr. Mary Healy, who since then has become a dear friend. I loved her testimony and sent it to everyone!

About this time, Jim Anderson at the *Coming Home Network* emailed and asked if there were any particular areas where I was struggling with regards to the Church. I dashed back an email, saying I thought the Church was great. But why do they have to make a big deal about Mary? He responded by sending me yet another book.

This one was *Hail, Holy Queen*, by Scott Hahn, a convert to Catholicism. I had read his earlier book, *Rome, Sweet Home*, and was intrigued that a Presbyterian had converted to Catholicism. But, still, not someone from my circles.

When *Hail, Holy Queen* arrived, I was immediately put off by the cover, which featured a very elaborate Renaissance-style

[6] On July 29, 2022, Bishop Barron was installed as the ninth bishop of the Diocese of Winona-Rochester, Minnesota.

portrait of the Virgin Mary, something I viewed at the time as pagan and idolatrous. I literally did *not* want anyone to see me reading that book, and even though it had a lot of thought-provoking content, I kept the cover covered up!

I was going to be home this particular weekend, and some leaders were coming to the house for dinner and a meeting. The house was all cleaned up, and food was cooking in the kitchen, making the house warm and inviting. I gave the house one final looking-over to make sure everything was in order, when I saw Scott Hahn's book on the floor next to my bed. I did not want everyone to see that I had *that* kind of "Catholic contraband" in my house! I swept by and kicked it under the bed!

I had had Catholic books, particularly books on the saints, in my house for years. But as Evangelicals, we had a particularly strong distrust of the Catholic Church's devotion to Mary, having been taught it was idolatry. And no one wanted to be accused of worshipping idols.

Up to this point, I never felt any pressure to join the Catholic Church. I knew that they were, indeed, Christians. However, I was not unhappy in the ministry or with my faith, and I was not looking to change anything. If anything, the ministries I was involved with were becoming more fruitful, and God was moving and working in people's lives like never before. I had connected with a leaders' network in Redding, California, and things were going well. But the incident with the book, *hiding it*, unsettled me. What was I doing? I realized I was not being honest, or transparent. Only a few people knew I was attending the Catechetical Institute, and even they, with the exception of the Kendricks in Virginia, were skeptical and more than a little scandalized.

I was ready to hit the brakes.

9

The Invitation

Evangelism is not so much about reminding people about how lost they are, but about how loved they are.

— Randall Worley

†

Over the years, I had taken many groups to the Holy Land to walk in the footsteps of Jesus in the land He called home. In 2012, I was getting our pilgrimage supplies all packed up for another trip. Sitting down to take a break, I glanced at the mail sitting next to my chair, and saw the monthly newsletter from the *Coming Home Network*. Usually, it was stapled, then folded in half and taped closed for mailing. But this one was all torn up from the mail machinery. So I picked it up, intending to refold it neatly. But when I opened it up, my eyes fell on the "Prayer List."

There, under the "clergy" column, I saw my own name. Alongside about twenty other names, I read, "Barbara, a full-time Word of Faith/Charismatic minister in St. Paul, Minnesota, as she discovers the Roman Catholic Church."

I sat and looked at it for a long time. *Were there really Catholics praying for me now?*

I had completed my first year of the Catechetical Institute, and I was determined to go ahead and finish the second year to complete the program. We had the entire summer off, and I would not begin my second year until September. In the meantime, I had a full calendar ahead of me. At the moment, I was in New Hampshire to speak at a conference.

Between meetings I checked my phone and was surprised to see a message from Debbie, "Please call." During the afternoon break, I went down to the river walk on the Merrimack River to call Debbie, as I wondered what was going on.

"Barbara!" I could hear the excitement in her voice. "We did it!"

"What's happening? What did you do?"

Debbie blurted, "We came into the Catholic Church!"

Instantly, a thought popped into my mind, *She beat me!!*

Debbie continued talking about how she and Bill got their marriage blessed, and how she and Bill and Shoshannah and the kids were all confirmed. And the whole time, I kept thinking, *She beat me.*

Debbie went on joyfully describing how they received Holy Communion, chatting about how beautiful it was, and how they were rejoicing in it, while all I could think was, "*She beat me*"? *Why would that be my first thought? What does this mean?*

I was happy for Debbie and Bill and the family, and after our call, I went back to finish up at the conference. I flew home from New Hampshire on Sunday, and when I awoke in my own bed on Monday morning, I lay there for a while, thinking about everything. Then I threw the covers off, and repeated to myself, *She beat me? Why would that be my reaction?* It was at that moment I realized that just maybe, possibly, perhaps ... I wanted to become Catholic before I die. Like in a couple of decades.

During the summer after my first year at the Catechetical Institute, I took a trip back to Virginia and spent several days at the home of the Kendricks, grilling Benoit with my never-ending questions. I had no problem with the Eucharist. Understanding Passover and knowing the Jewish roots of the Eucharist, I understood the eternal nature of Communion, and I had come to believe in the Real Presence. I did bristle at the idea that a priest was needed for the Consecration, but Benoit gently explained it to me again and showed me Holy Orders in Scripture, and then he spent hours leading us in songs of worship to the Lord and sharing his love of the Church with me.

After talking for hours, I couldn't seem to help coming back to what I'd been taught about Mary, and Benoit said something to me that just suddenly clicked. "Barbara," he said, "Scripture tells us that Jesus only did what the Father showed Him to do." I nodded in agreement. "So here is Jesus Christ on the Cross, only doing what the Father shows Him to do, saying, 'Behold your mother.'"

"Now, the Protestant view dismisses this moment," he continued, "as though Jesus were saying, 'Oh, John, I almost forgot! Can you watch out for my mom?' Almost an afterthought, while He was in the midst of the eternal work of the Cross for all mankind. But that's not how Catholics for thousands of years have understood it."

Benoit was on the edge of his seat, and I can still see his dark eyes bright with love and passion. "What Jesus did in that moment when He said from the Cross, 'Woman, behold, your son!' and then to John, 'Behold, your mother!' was to give His Mother to the Church. Jesus was entrusting the disciples, and John, and all of us to Mary. It was not an afterthought."

I could instantly see that this was as Jesus was completing His sacrifice and that it could not be separated from it. I still didn't understand all the theology of it—I had avoided it up till then! But my heart changed in that moment.

September arrived, and it was time to start the second and last year of my program at the Catechetical Institute. Once again, we were gathered at St. Mary's Chapel at the St. Paul Seminary on the campus of St. Thomas University for our opening Mass, and to witness our instructors make their vows to be true to the teaching of the Roman Catholic Church. I was even more moved the second time. And this time, I participated in the Mass, going forward with arms crossed to receive a blessing.

Jeff Cavins had warned me that I might find the second year of CI a little more challenging, as it was focusing much more on the traditions, but I found that I had begun to be able to "trust the Church" and remain open and not get so "combative" when I didn't agree with something. But the big thing that happened was my small group.

As second-year students, we were assigned to new groups, and my small group that second year could not have been more different from my first-year group. My first group was larger and pretty quiet and stayed on topic religiously! My second group was smaller, chatty, fun, and "went with the flow." In group one we didn't talk about anything outside of the class. Group two wanted to know each person's name, where we were from, which parish we attended, what we did ... and in my case, "Why do you occasionally miss a night?" So I went ahead and whispered to them that I was not Catholic and shared just a little bit about myself.

Soon, when my group gathered, we'd have a quick discussion on that week's topic, and then they'd want to know where I was "at." I don't remember all of their names, but I remember all of their open and friendly faces, and I definitely remember Dave and Sharon Altman, the couple in the group. All of them were doing something I had never witnessed in all the Catholic churches I had visited over the years. They were practicing the three rules of evangelism on me.

Rule 1: Invite.
Rule 2: Invite.
Rule 3: Invite.

They told me they were praying for me and my "journey." I didn't even realize until then that I'd been on a journey! One young woman gave me the book *Unbound*, which she said had changed her life. Another gave me something called a Miraculous Medal and a rosary, which I was a little skeptical about but graciously received from her. Another took me to NET (National Evangelization Teams) events, held at the NET headquarters not far from both of our homes. And they would all invite me to Mass at their churches.

One day, after our Monday night lecture from the third part of the *Catechism* (Life in Christ), and our brief group discussion, Dave Altman suggested that I might enjoy something called RCIA (Rite of Christian Initiation for Adults).[7] He and his wife gave me a piece of paper with Randy Mueller's name and phone number on it and suggested I give him a call.

It was one thing to attend a NET meeting that was just a few blocks away or to accept a book that was lovingly offered to me, but to call Randy about taking another class? Besides, the "Rite of Christian Initiation for Adults" sounded a little too serious for me. On top of all that, I was busy! My eldest daughter and her kids had moved into my house, and in addition to being Mom and Grandma under one roof, I was still as busy as ever with ministry.

[7] In 2021, this process of initiating non-Catholic adults into the Catholic faith and the sacramental life of the Church was changed from "RCIA" to "OCIA" (Order of Christian Initiation for Adults).

Every Monday I would go to class, and every Monday Dave and Sharon would ask if I had gotten in touch with Randy. And every week, I would tell them that I was sorry, but I had not had the time. Dave looked at me very deeply one day and gently said, "I think you should give him a call."

Soon it was December. I had just flown in from the East Coast and picked up my car from the Minneapolis airport and was heading to our class. According to my classmates, RCIA had started back in September and had been in session for several months. As I was driving, I was thinking, *I know they are going to ask me if I called Randy. I just can't keep telling them that I didn't have time . . . again.*

While at a stop light, I reached into my purse, and there was the paper with Randy's name and number on it. I thought to myself, *I'll just call quick.... I know they started months ago.... I'll tell him I might be interested in next year's class.* I called the number, and soon I was talking to Randy. "I've been waiting to hear from you!" he said, as I winced. I told him that I knew RCIA started a while ago, and he said, "That's no problem, it sounds like you already know a lot about the Church anyway. What are you doing on Thursday?"

I can still see the snowy, unplowed side street I was driving down. I hesitated. I wasn't doing anything that Thursday! And then, I took the step, and just like that, I was signed up for RCIA, at Nativity of Our Lord Catholic Church in St. Paul, Minnesota. And now, I couldn't wait to see Dave and Sharon and the rest of my group.

10

The Power of Grace

The transformation of the heart that leads us to confess our sins is a gift from God.... It is "His" work.

— Pope Francis

✝

I began attending RCIA regularly at Nativity of Our Lord Catholic Church. There were several others in my class, and we met in what looked like a library. Randy, our RCIA director, was enthusiastic and a good teacher. I still remember learning about the Catholic Church's yearly calendar of seasons and feast days and learning about how to become Catholic, though at that time I had no intention of actually becoming confirmed.

My ministry work was accelerating, and I was making plans for an extended mission to Brazil in the fall. But I felt like I was at a crossroads. We were seeing the Lord move in the lives of so many people. I was taking people on mission trips to other countries, and we praised God together for how He used us to make a difference in people's lives. At the same time, I was a second-year student at the Catechetical Institute *and* I was attending RCIA. Although I had delayed even contemplating coming into the Roman Catholic Church, it was apparent for a while now that a decision needed to be made. I flew out to Virginia and visited the Kendricks, who prayed with me, and my old spiritual father and mentor, Rev. Chappell, who had prayed with me for so many years.

Brother Chappell listened patiently as I told him my "Catholic story." He already knew parts of it, and he asked me a few questions; then he told me he wanted time to pray about it and that we could get together the next day. I could tell he was sympathetic to what was going on in my life. But I was very surprised when the next day came and he told me that I must obey God and follow where He was leading!

Whoa! I began to tell him all the reasons I shouldn't even begin thinking of going into the Catholic Church, but he just smiled and told me to keep following Jesus!

I was relieved, but somehow nervous at the same time. People like me did not become Catholic. I had given my life to my Lord and was a missionary, an evangelist. Jesus was not a part of my life, He *was* my life! Should I lay down my ministry, and with it my yes to God to be His instrument, so that I could become Catholic? Is that really what God was saying to me? It seemed impossible.

I met Jeff Heil while speaking at a meeting, and when I found out he was Catholic, I sent him copies of some of the books I was reading. I shared a little with him about attending the Catechetical Institute, and that I had come to love the Roman Catholic Church, but I was more than a little conflicted. He arranged a meeting with a priest named Fr. Starbuck at the American Martyrs Retreat House in Iowa (which has since closed its doors).

Fr. Starbuck listened as I told him my story and then asked to pray with me. Finally, leaning forward with great excitement, he said, "Barbara, there's really no big decision here! The Church says you *are* Catholic. You've always been Catholic since you were baptized." I could hardly believe what he was telling me! I felt like I'd been hit with a ton of bricks! I didn't remember anyone else saying that to me. "You're already Catholic, Barbara!" And he encouraged me to come "home."

"But what about all the people I'm ministering to and sharing the gospel with?"

"Obedience will only bring blessing," he said with a soft smile. And from that time on, he said it to me often, "You're Catholic! There's no big decision here!" and "Obedience will only bring blessing." And then he told me that he believed I would be a "bridge" for non-Catholic Christians to come and understand the Church! I shook my head at that one!

I drove home, thinking about what Fr. Starbuck said to me, and what my longtime friend and mentor, Brother Chappell, said to me. It seemed like I was at the point of no return. But I just could not imagine what would happen if I actually took the next step.

Fr. Starbuck said I was already Catholic, to come home, and that obedience would only bring blessing. Brother Chappell told me to keep following Jesus. The question was now, could I really follow where He seemed to be leading me?

I returned home, to my office, to my work, and to my classes. At the Catechetical Institute, we were required to attend "Formation Days" in order to graduate, and the one that Saturday was about the Sacrament of Reconciliation. Ah, one of the sacraments of the Church that I was still sure was not necessary. I mean, I could go straight to Jesus! As I prepared to go to the morning formation, my mind was made up. Along with ministry responsibilities, *this* was why I would not become Catholic. With that settled in my heart, I drove to the Saturday formation.

I arrived and settled into my seat. There, I was ready. I didn't need to go to a priest for forgiveness! I had Jesus! I will just listen, check the class off my list of requirements for graduation, which was getting close, and be done with it! There! Decision made! *I have to leave early anyway to get to Fargo, where I'll be speaking tonight,* I thought to myself.

A priest named Fr. Steven Hoffman was leading the formation class. He came in carrying a picture with the back turned toward us, and then, after prayer, he began. "It is Jesus you are coming to in Reconciliation," he said, turning the picture around to reveal a beautiful print of a painting of Jesus, with His Hands outstretched: *Jesus: The Friend of Sinners.*

Of course, I was moved immediately. As Fr. Hoffman unpacked the Catholic teaching on Reconciliation, all my doubts began to melt away. I knew that Jesus was my Savior, that He had borne my sins, my rebellion, my "wanting what I wanted" in my life, upon Himself. He bore my pride, my stubbornness, sins I hadn't even committed yet, and the consequences of every tiny act of defiance.

Fr. Hoffman was speaking, "The Risen Savior told the apostles, the same way the Father sent Me, I am now sending you, 'Those sins you forgive are forgiven.' The apostles, the first priests of Christ, received the ability to reconcile men and women to our Heavenly Father and the community of faith on the very day that Jesus was risen. In Confession, when I go to that priest, he is acting *in persona Christi*, in the very *Person* of Christ."

As he forgives sins, the priest represents *Jesus*. My mind went instantly to all the people around the world whom I had ministered to over the years. I had wanted to represent Christ to them, to help them experience the living love of God. I could see that the priests, "in persona Christi," were the connection between God and the people, bringing them to the love of Jesus. And that in going to the priest in Confession, I was, in truth, going to Jesus.

I often wondered about certain verses that I tended to "spiritualize" (rather than take literally) if they did not match my preconceived theological ideas. Right there in the class, I could *see* the beautiful story of John 20:23, where Jesus commissioned His apostles after He had risen from the dead: "If you forgive the sins of any, they are forgiven; if you retain the sins of any, they are retained." He had just breathed on them and said, "Receive the Holy Spirit" (20:22). The disciples were commissioned, not to forgive sins by *their* authority, but by God's. And with it came great responsibility.

This passage dovetailed with Matthew 16:19, where the Lord says to Simon, whom He just renamed Peter, "I will give you the keys of the kingdom of heaven, and whatever you bind on earth shall be bound in heaven, and whatever you loose on earth shall be loosed in heaven."

I could see it so clearly. After all the years of research and reading, praying, and questioning. The whole gospel that I loved, and had been sharing with others, was in the Catholic Church. He had given tangible people, the priests, as a physical representation of Himself. No matter the state of the priest, clean or unclean, God was honoring His own Word as He acted through His priesthood to bring people to Himself.

Fr. Hoffman continued sharing the loving theology of the Church. "Yes, there are people who experience forgiveness because of their faith in Christ who are not Catholic and have not gone to Reconciliation, for while Jesus had bound Himself *to* His sacraments, He Himself was not bound *by* those sacraments."

Listening, I suddenly realized why I had been so resistant to the idea of receiving the sacraments: I had been worried that if I accepted the Church's teachings of the Sacrament of Reconciliation, I was also accepting that Christians outside of the Church, including my friends, family, and colleagues, were not Christians at all! And I knew that wasn't true.

But as I listened, I also realized something else: this was not what the Church teaches. And I was relieved. The *Catechism*, which I was studying, says this:

> "All who have been justified by faith in Baptism are incorporated into Christ; they therefore have a right to be called Christians, and with good reason are accepted as brothers in the Lord by the children of the Catholic Church." ... Christ's Spirit uses these Churches and ecclesial communities as means of salvation, whose power *derives from the fullness of grace and truth that Christ has entrusted to the Catholic Church*. All these blessings come from Christ and lead to him and are in themselves calls to "Catholic unity." (818–819, citing *Unitatis Redintegratio* 3 and *Lumen Gentium* 8)

Reading these words, it dawned on me that all the Catholics who had been praying for me all this time, and whom I had known all along the way, acknowledged that I was already a Christian. Now, I was being invited into *fullness*.

Soon the lines began to form for Confession, and no one dared leave without first going to Reconciliation. I now ached to participate. I asked someone, "I'm not in the Church, but can I go to Reconciliation too?" They said yes ... and I got in the shortest line. But the line was still long and slow, and I had an appointment in Fargo. So, I slipped away and began the four-hour drive, wondering what was happening in my life as I went.

11

Just Another Step

At each fork you must make a decision.

— C. S. Lewis

†

So many answers to so many questions. But, after meetings in Fargo that same weekend, all I felt was sorrow. How could I lay down the ministry and stop serving people by bringing the message of Jesus and His Kingdom? I laid my life down and gave myself to Christ and His gospel. How do I turn my back on that? What would people think?

Over and over in my mind, on my way back to the Cities, my thoughts returned to Luke 9:62, "No one who puts his hand to the plow and looks back is fit for the kingdom of God." I knew there were different ways to "put your hand to the plow" in God's vineyard, but I had been taught a certain way, and I had said yes to a certain calling. I prayed all the way home, surrendering my life to Jesus, giving Him my all, asking the Lord to show me if I was being deceived by the Catholic Church.

On Monday, I was back at the Catechetical Institute. Jeff Cavins was present although there was a different presenter that night, and I went up to him after class. He was probably thinking, *What now?* I had pestered him with questions, challenges really, arguments disguised as questions, throughout my time at the CI.

"Okay, Jeff, I believe," I began. "I believe in the Eucharist, all of it! But wouldn't it be selfish of me to stop doing everything I'm doing so that I can receive the Eucharist?"

And without batting an eye he answered me, "I would think that if the Lord invited you into a deep place of intimacy, you wouldn't want to tell Him you had better things to do."

Bam! That was it! I was stricken. There was nothing better in the universe than to receive Him, Body, Blood, Soul, and Divinity! There was *nothing* more important!

I got into my car, and on the way home, I kept saying to myself, *I think I have to become Catholic*. And by the time I got home, such joy welled up inside of me that I was laughing and crying at the same time. "I think I have to become Catholic!!" It wasn't about a choice between churches I was making. It was obedience that I was choosing. Obedience would only bring blessing.

I prayed and pondered everything that God had been speaking to my heart. I looked back over the years and could see His Hand and guidance. And Jeff Cavin's words continued to ring in my ears. I spoke with Brother Chappell over the phone and Debbie Kendrick, and told them what was happening. I was going to choose obedience. It might sting at first, but it will only bring blessing.

But first things first. It was time to let my ministry board know what was going on.

I had confided earlier in a few of my closest friends, who were quizzical but trusting, about some of the things I was learning about the Church. But now word was getting out, and I gathered with my board and others who had been part of the ministry who wanted me to explain what was going on.

I began to tell of my journey, of finding out that the saints of the early Catholic Church were deep believers, of being at the back of the Catholic church during the conference outside of

Philadelphia where Jesus Christ Himself was standing right in front of me, only to open my eyes and discover the priest holding the monstrance over me. I shared about finding out I was baptized in the Catholic Church, and this must be why Jesus had always been with me, even before I realized He was my Savior and my God, when I was born again. I continued, sharing about the churches I visited and the questions I asked, and that finally … *finally*, I had decided to follow where He was leading me. Right into the Roman Catholic Church.

One dear friend said, "Yes, it does sound like that's where God is leading you." The rest of my friends were sympathetic but confused and probably glad it wasn't them.

No one knew what to do with me, or this news. Some people stopped speaking to me, cutting off long relationships. There were churches that began "uninviting" me, which I expected, and I was not able to find fault with anyone for their confusion, or sense of betrayal. I understood. I still understand. I was labeled a heretic, and it was announced that I had succumbed to a "religious spirit," which was about the worst thing you could say in those circles!

Still, I understood. I was coming into the Roman Catholic Church and of course, decoupling from another. My livelihood was tied to it. I'd always known what I was doing the next day. I had a team and people whom I was training. But not anymore. The ministry trip to Brazil was canceled, churches canceled. There were still a few meetings that asked me to speak, but not many. I didn't know what was going to happen, but I had to keep going. I was also nearing the last of my funds from the sale of my house on the river. Now, I was in God's Hands.

With that difficult task done, I made an appointment with Fr. Hoffman, who invited me to come out to his church in Clearwater, west of the Twin Cities, to see him. It was there that I had my first

Sacrament of Reconciliation. I asked him where I should begin, since I had been a Christian for a long time and had experienced a definite time of repentance when I first heard the gospel and came to God. He very gently suggested, "From the beginning." I felt sheepish and self-conscious at first, but soon the words were spilling out. I wanted to confess it all. My heart was light and filled with joy. And I thought in that moment, that somehow, without knowing it before, I was where I had always wanted to be.

When Fr. Hoffman spoke and absolved me of my (many) sins, it was as if the ocean had settled into a deep calm. Peace filled me. I was coming home.

Fr. Hoffman took me into the sanctuary and taught me how and when to kneel, how and when to bless myself with holy water, and how to do the sign of the cross, basically showing me the ropes of participating in the life of what was becoming my new community.

Soon it was time for the Rite of Sending, and I took what I considered a giant step toward the Church. Randy Mueller and the rest of our class and I sat in a single row at the great Cathedral of St. Paul. As the service commenced, I looked around this place that I had grown to love. I had passed so many hours under its great dome, praying and meditating on the Lord, moved by the beauty. Never would I have dreamed that I would be sitting there in this church as part of the Church, and yet here I was! And I knew that my Lord Jesus always knew.

12

Not Exactly According to Plan

I feel the rains of your love,
Feel the winds of your Spirit,
Now the heartbeat of heaven
Let us hear.[8]

—Jesus Culture

[8] "Let It Rain" from *Come Away*, Jesus Culture. Lyrics by Michael Farren. © 2010.

†

Later that week, I received an email from Fr. Starbuck, inviting me to be part of a pilgrimage group he was taking to Rome for the Easter Vigil. He suggested that I could receive my First Communion and Confirmation there! I said that I would be thrilled of course, and asked how I would arrange that, since I was scheduled to receive these sacraments at the Easter Vigil at Nativity of Our Lord Catholic Church. Randy checked with the archbishop, who said I could receive Communion at the Easter Vigil in Rome, but that I must be confirmed at my local church, and we arranged a later date for my Confirmation.

I had believed that the Eucharist was the Body, Blood, Soul, and Divinity of Jesus for a while, and now I was going to Rome for my first Catholic Communion to receive this visible sign of an invisible grace! I finally would not just be eating a cracker and drinking grape juice and thinking about Jesus and the price He paid for my sins, but I would be partaking of the consecrated bread and wine, receiving His Body and His Blood, uniting me to the Body of Christ!

I had been to Rome many times as a non-Catholic missionary-evangelist. The same Rome that I looked down my nose at when we approached the Vatican and its statues and prayers. But this time, I was full of wonder.

On this pilgrimage, I marveled at everything I had missed when I had been there before. One of my favorite places was the Basilica of Saint Paul Outside the Walls, and of course, St. Peter's Basilica.

While at St. Peter's, we had some time before a Mass to walk around on our own. I went to the side where some confessionals were set up and found a booth for people who spoke English. The line was very short, which I found surprising. Above the confessionals was an altar, the Altar of the Navicella, literally, "little ship," above which was a large painting of Peter on the water with Jesus, gripping Peter's wrist, pulling him atop the stormy waters. *That's me,* I thought to myself, eyeing the waves in the great painting.

It was my turn at the English speakers' confessional. This would be only my second Confession, and I wouldn't have Fr. Hoffman to coach me. I heard an Irish brogue from the other side of a screen. It's hard to talk to someone you can't see! I told him I was coming into the Church and would be having my First Communion at the Vigil, and that I would be confirmed later in the month. I told him I was leaving my work for the Lord so I could come into full communion with the Catholic Church, and that although I knew that God had led me to this moment, I was still a little anxious about doing the right thing.

Afterward he led me out of the confessional and, taking me by the hand, and with the other hand pointing to the painting, he said, "You must obey the Lord's call to come out of your boat. The Lord promises to *grip* you, and you will remain in His grip, as you walk with Him on this water." I found this profoundly moving, that the Lord would arrange for *that* priest to be there, under *that* painting, which indeed, perfectly depicted how I was feeling as I was stepping out of the boat.

†

It was March 2013, the first Easter Vigil for the new Pope Francis from Argentina. Rome was packed with joyful pilgrims from all over South America and the world. It felt a bit overcrowded! We toured all the usual Catholic pilgrim sites, and I walked around St. Peter's for hours, wondering why I had refused to visit it before, and how was it that I ever thought it was pagan? I could not help feeling a deep connection with it all.

Finally, on the morning of the Easter Vigil, Fr. Starbuck handed each pilgrim a ticket and reminded us that, even with the ticket, we needed to be there six or eight hours early! Someone said, "Let's go *now*"! So a few of us headed to the Vatican from the pilgrim guest house, and the rest took off to see more of Rome, arranging to meet up later in the day. I went with the first group—I was not taking any chances. I just had to get in! I was going to receive Communion! Fr. Starbuck was one of the servers for the Mass that night, and as soon as he received the consecrated host, he was going to come to me.

We got to St. Peter's Square, and there were already several hundred people in line! This was before noon! I couldn't believe it and was so very glad I'd chosen to get there early. The line behind me was growing, and so was the line in front of me! But it wasn't growing the right way! It was getting wider and wider!

While we waited, I struck up a conversation with the woman behind me. She was an American United Nations employee who worked at the Rome office. She was sharing a little about her life, and suddenly, I could just "see" it, and I asked her, "Is your back hurting?" And I pointed to where I believed her pain was. "I am never without pain," she said somberly. I asked her if I could pray with her. "Here?" she asked. "Yes, right here." And then spreading my arms toward the Basilica, I said, "What better place could there be?" So, we prayed, and she said the pain was gone.

Surprised, she said, "I can't believe it!" We stood there all afternoon, and she began going up and down the growing and thickening line to greet friends and work colleagues. All afternoon I kept hearing her voice over all the other voices, "I can't believe it! The pain is still gone!" And she would bring me her friends who wanted prayer. And that is how I spent my time in the line at St. Peter's Square.

Hours later, when the guards were getting ready to open security screening, she told me, "Everyone is going to run once they get through security and the gates. You're going to have to run, or you will get run over!"

I didn't believe her. "They're going to run?"

"Just stay with me!" she said. "And if anyone tries to talk to you in Italian, just pretend you don't understand them!"

"That's easy," I said.

Sure enough, the gates opened and the crowd (which had ceased being in any kind of line hours ago) swelled both behind me and in front of me, and began surging forward. The heavens opened and a heavy, cold rain began to fall. Thousands of umbrellas opened, and because we were jammed together, the water from the tops of the umbrellas had nowhere to go but poured like rivers down our backs and faces.

I was soaked and cold, and the crowd continued to surge forward. It was crazy, and I was surprised that so many people were so desperate to get inside. And my new friend was right, people began running for all they were worth toward the doors of St. Peter's once they got through the gates. It was amazing to behold: thousands of people running into the Basilica! I don't know, I was expecting something a little more dignified, but it made me happy to see people running to the Church!

Then it was our turn, and yes, I ran all the way in. The woman from the line led me a different way than the other pilgrims were going, to a seat right behind the altar, on the second row. I was soaked to the skin and shivering, and I still had my ticket. No one ever asked me for it! Later I found out that only four of the pilgrims from our group, even though everybody had tickets, were able to get inside!

As long as I live, I will never forget the sight and experience of the darkened basilica and the sudden silence, with a golden glow beginning to shine through a far doorway, and then the emerging of the new pontiff, as the light of candles being lit spread across the church, until it was all aglow, brightening the church and the faces of tens of thousands of people.

I had lost sight of Fr. Starbuck, and when it was time, I received my First Communion from a priest I didn't know. It didn't matter. I had received *Him*!

The next day was Easter Sunday, and the crowd at St. Peter's Square reached all the way to Castel Sant'Angelo! We had learned our lesson the day before, and our group was right at the front of St. Peter's Square. When the new pope, Pope Francis, appeared in the balcony, the crowd of people from every corner of the world began shouting, "Papa Francesco! Papa Francesco!" It went on and on! And finally I was shouting too, "Papa Francesco!" until I was sobbing and could no longer speak. Someone in the group asked later why I was crying so hard. Was it exhaustion and excitement from the day before? It was neither of those things. I had realized I had a really big family, and with it came a father, and I was surprised by the sudden awareness of this.

We soon left Rome and went to Medjugorje for the last few days of our trip before returning to the States. I came home full. So much had happened in just the past few months. The Holy Spirit had moved on my heart in so many ways.

I was more than ready for what was to come. Just a few weeks later, on April 27, 2013, I was driving to the Saturday morning Mass at Nativity of Our Lord Catholic Church in St. Paul, Minnesota, ready to receive the "seal" at the Rite of Confirmation. My daughter Sarah was in attendance, as well as some of my RCIA classmates who had already been received into the Church, and Randy. While in prayer, I sensed the joy of my "friend" St. Teresa of Avila and other beloved saints, and I thought of The Man in the Sky, and the baptism I didn't know I'd received. I thought of the journey of being a wife, a mother, an evangelist, a pastor. And I smiled.

> The kingdom of heaven is like a merchant in search of fine pearls, who on finding one pearl of great value, went and sold all that he had and bought it. (Matt. 13:45–46)

I had found the pearl of great price. And it was true, as Fr. Starbuck had said, obedience would only bring blessing. The Holy Spirit knew this day was coming before I'd ever taken a breath. It wasn't because I had merely studied or simply changed my views or interpretations of long-fought theological issues that I found myself reciting the Creed and kneeling at the exaltation of the Host. It was because, step by step, I followed Him, wanting, like the apostle John, to be so close to my Lord and my God that I could lay my head upon His Shoulder. I followed Him in a journey that continually led me into His Heart.

I didn't know that day what was ahead, and I still don't. But that doesn't matter. I was following Him to a home I never knew I had. My heart was satisfied.

Epilogue

I did not know it at the time, but within a year I would end up marrying Jeff Heil and moving to Iowa. No one was more surprised than me that I would end up being an Iowa farmer's wife! Everything in my life was new and different. I had a new Church, lived in a new state, and had a new name!

That same year, 2014, I was invited by Kelly Wahlquist from the Catechetical Institute to gather with some Catholic women in Jackson Hole, Wyoming, where I met Catholic women in different aspects of ministry from all over the country. They were beautiful, talented, Catholic women of deep faith! Many lasting friendships were formed during that week at the Grand Tetons, and I would return several times. One of the women I met was the sweetest southern belle from Arkansas, Christy Miller, who invited me to come and speak for a conference in Arkansas the following summer. Besides sharing my conversion story in a home outside of St. Paul after I first came into the Church, this would be the first time for me to speak and minister at a conference after becoming Catholic. Little did I know that it was only the beginning, and that I would go on to found *From His Heart Ministries*.

Since then, Jeff and I together have been to sixteen countries to share the gospel. In addition to that, I have been to nineteen countries with Lloyd and Nancy Greenhaw, either with *Renewal Ministries* or on our own, as God has opened doors I could not have imagined.

After being in Rome for the Easter Vigil, our pilgrimage group continued on to Medjugorje. The entire time I was there the Holy Spirit kept telling me to buy a statue of the Holy Mother for my mother. I resisted. It was one thing to come into the Church and accept that Mary was the Mother of God (and not just the mother of Jesus) but, in my mind at least, it was another thing for me to go and buy a statue of her.

As I walked the streets and lanes and climbed Apparition Hill and sat in adoration at St. James Church, the Holy Spirit kept prompting me to get a statue. Finally, with less than an hour before it was time to get on the bus to get to the airport and go home, I found myself running through the pension where we were staying, calling out, "Can someone open the store? I have to get a statue of the Holy Mother for my mother!" I bought two.

That fall, I gave my mother one of the statues of the Holy Mother while she was visiting for my youngest daughter's wedding. A few weeks later I called her at her home in Washington. "I've got her on the mantel," she said. "Mom, who's on the mantel?" "Mary! I've got her on the mantel!"

"Mary's not on your mantel!" I corrected her. "A *statue* of Mary is on your mantel!"

Then she said, "I've started RCIA! And I've gone to Confession!"

"Mom, that's awesome!"

A couple of years later, when my brother Bob and I were helping our mother take my stepfather's ashes to be buried in his boyhood home in Kansas, we decided to see if we could find our old house in Olathe where we had once lived when I was a child. Mom remembered right where it was. We sat a respectable distance away (no one wants a carful of strangers looking into their house). Then we got out and looked around and I said, "Mom, which side of the house was my bedroom on? This is where I was when I first saw The Man in the Sky."

My mom chuckled and pointed at the back of the house. "Oh, you talked about him so much that finally your dad went out to see who was in our backyard and looking in your window!"

"It was Jesus, Mom!" She looked at me and said, "Who else could it be?"

When she got back home, my mother, Pam, received Holy Communion for the first time in over fifty years!

I told her later, when we were sharing what God was doing in our lives, "Thank you, Mom, for bringing me to God."

"When did I bring you to God?"

"When you had me baptized, you brought me to God!"

And she said, "Aww, and thank *you* for bringing me back to God."

Although Mom's grandmother had died back in the 1970s, her prayers had been answered. For the Lord never forgets a prayer.

A Final Thought

Did you know that God has a plan for your life, and that the Lord wants you to experience a closer and more intimate relationship with Him? I shared my story here, first and foremost, to show you how God works in the lives of His children to bring healing, forgiveness, and joy! And what God has done for me, He wants to give to you as well.

Don't worry if you haven't prayed this way before or aren't sure how to begin listening for God's voice. You can offer this prayer anywhere—in a church or adoration chapel, or in a quiet corner at home. The Lord wants to speak to His children, and the Holy Spirit is faithful to build on the graces we receive at Baptism and Confirmation. Don't be afraid to surrender and open your heart to what He has to say. God bless you as you begin this wonderful "Journey into His Heart"!

Prayer of Invitation

Father in Heaven, thank You for sending Your Son, Jesus, to die for my sins.

Dear Lord Jesus, You said You are standing at the door of my heart knocking, and that if I open that door,

You will come into me, and dine with me, and I with You. Right now, I open the door and invite You into my heart. I surrender my life to You and ask You to be the Lord of my life, my King, and my God. I confess that You, Jesus, are my Savior, and I repent and turn away from my sins, and anything in my life that is not pleasing to You. I choose You.

Thank You, Lord, for loving me, and going to the cross and dying for my salvation. Guide me, Lord, and help me follow You in every area of my life.

In the Holy Name of Jesus. Amen.

Questions for Group Discussion or Personal Reflection

As you read this story, were there parts that resonated with you in a special way? You may want to go back and underline or highlight these passages or write your questions or thoughts in the margins. Ask the Lord what He wants to show you about your own life through this story. If you aren't sure how to begin, don't worry! The following questions may be used to prime the pump for fruitful reflection or small-group conversation.

1. What are some of the themes or ideas that stood out to you as you read Barbara's story? Are there parts of her story that particularly resonate with your own life?
2. Barbara's childhood experiences were often difficult, yet she also received special graces that ultimately led her into the Church. What are some examples of these graces? What are some of your earliest memories of God at work in you?
3. The Holy Spirit gave Barbara special gifts to help others find healing and forgiveness in Christ—including her parents. Do you have relationships in need of healing?

4. Early on, Barbara was taught to believe that Catholics are not "real" Christians. Did you learn anything from Barbara's testimony that will help you in your conversation with non-Catholic Christians?
5. If someone asked you to share your testimony, what would you say?
6. Barbara identified several Church Fathers and other saints whose writings were important to her faith journey. This "holy habit" of spiritual reading ultimately led her to go back to school for catechetical formation. Why is it important to continue learning about the faith as adults? What would you like to learn?
7. Barbara's story shows us how the Holy Spirit works in us to transform not just our minds (how we think) but our hearts as well (how we relate to God and others). Why are both kinds of conversion important?
8. How does the Holy Spirit speak to you? Can you recall a time when the Lord asked you to do something? What happened?
9. Throughout the book, Barbara returns to her objection about Catholics worshipping "idols." How are the images of saints—and of Jesus and the Holy Family—helpful to deepening our faith? How would you explain this to someone who thought they were "idols"?
10. Barbara's life was radically changed the day she first encountered Christ in the monstrance, in the eucharistic procession. Has the Lord ever moved your heart or spoken to you through His presence in the Eucharist—either at Mass, or in adoration? Are you willing to ask Him to open your eyes and heart, and reveal Himself to you?

Sophia Institute

Sophia Institute is a nonprofit institution that seeks to nurture the spiritual, moral, and cultural life of souls and to spread the gospel of Christ in conformity with the authentic teachings of the Roman Catholic Church.

Sophia Institute Press fulfills this mission by offering translations, reprints, and new publications that afford readers a rich source of the enduring wisdom of mankind.

Sophia Institute also operates the popular online resource CatholicExchange.com. *Catholic Exchange* provides world news from a Catholic perspective as well as daily devotionals and articles that will help readers to grow in holiness and live a life consistent with the teachings of the Church.

In 2013, Sophia Institute launched Sophia Teachers to renew and rebuild Catholic culture through service to Catholic education. With the goal of nurturing the spiritual, moral, and cultural life of souls, and an abiding respect for the role and work of teachers, we strive to provide materials and programs that are at once enlightening to the mind and ennobling to the heart; faithful and complete, as well as useful and practical.

Sophia Institute gratefully recognizes the Solidarity Association for preserving and encouraging the growth of our apostolate over the course of many years. Without their generous and timely support, this book would not be in your hands.

www.SophiaInstitute.com
www.CatholicExchange.com
www.SophiaTeachers.org

Sophia Institute Press® is a registered trademark of Sophia Institute.
Sophia Institute is a tax-exempt institution as defined by the
Internal Revenue Code, Section 501(c)(3). Tax ID 22-2548708.